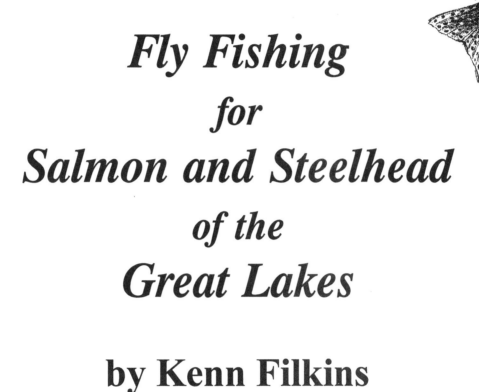

Fly Fishing
for
Salmon and Steelhead
of the
Great Lakes

by Kenn Filkins

Wilderness Adventure Books

About the Author

A native of Michigan, Kenn Filkins has fished all over the Great Lakes region, and has caught steelhead in every month of the year. He has spent the past six years researching the most productive fly fishing techniques of successful guides throughout the Great Lakes rivers. He has traveled to Great Lakes rivers in both the U.S. and Ontario to experiment with the tips and techniques he decribes in this book. Filkins has written extensively about fly fishing in regional and national magazines, including *American Angler, Sports Afield, Salmon, Trout, Steelheader, Flyfishing,* and *Michigan Out-of-Doors.*

Kenn is the Senior Minister of the First Church of Christ in Sault Ste. Marie, Michigan. A popular seminar speaker, he teaches workshops on outdoor writing and other topics. He's received national acclaim for his inspirational books, including *Comfort Those Who Mourn, A Comforting Word: Encouraging a Grieving Friend, Seven Sayings One Friday,* and *Characters of Calvary.*

A lifelong outdoorsman, Kenn has been an active falconer since 1979, and edited *A Bond With The Wild*, an anthology of falconry stories.

He shares his love of the outdoors with his two sons, Micaiah and Andrew.

To my two favorite fishing partners
my sons
Micaiah and Andrew

LCCN: 96-44535
ISBN: 0-923568-42-5

Illustrations by Martha Diebboll, David Harbaugh, Brian Ruzzo, and Elizabeth Yelland

Cover Design by Advanced Images

Wilderness Adventure Books
P.O. Box 576
Chelsea, MI 48116

Library of Congress Cataloging-in-Publication Data

Filkins, Kenn.
    Fly fishing for salmon and steelhead of the Great Lakes / Kenn Filkins.
    Includes index.
    ISBN 0-923568-42-5
    1. Salmon fishing—Great lakes. 2. Steelhead fishing—Great Lakes. 3.
Fly fishing—Great Lakes.   I. Title.
SH684.F54   1998
799. 1'756'0977—dc21   96-44535
                                    CIP

Manufactured in the United States of America

Contents

Acknowledgements

This book would not be possible without the encouragement, insight and assistance of my family and many friends.

I openly thank all the steelhead and salmon fly fishing guides for their advice, guidance, instruction and stories; without them this book would not be valuable. Specifically, I am especially grateful to Jim and Tom Johnson; their keen insight and friendship have been a source of fly fishing wisdom through the years. I highly regard John Hunter for his genuine and warm character, and for sharing the joy of the river with me. I thank Bob Nicholson for his historical insight and his candor.

I also thank my fly fishing and fly tying partners, with whom I have shared so many delightful days fishing and tying. I deeply appreciate my two sons: Micaiah (I Kings 22), "Mack" for his laughter and spirit of adventure, and Andrew (John 1), "Drew" for his quick wit and artistic insight. I thank especially my best friends, Tom Jared and Al Renner, for each day we spend on the river, tying or talking. I express my appreciation to my friend and fly tying professional, John Kilmer, for his patience, instruction and willingness to innovate in fly tying. I give special thanks to my brother, Leroy, who says, "Kenn only has me around for sermon illustrations and fishing anecdotes." Trust me, it's a lot more than that.

I thank Wilderness Adventure Books for publishing this book and my editor, Erin Sims Howarth, for her hard effort, excitement and unending encouragement with this project.

Introduction—The *Whole* Truth

Until now, the story of Great Lakes fly fishing for steelhead and salmon has never been fully told. This is curious because the Great Lakes region comprises several major scenes of the North American tapestry of salmon and steelhead fishing. It is often stated that one third of the anglers in America live in the states that border the Great Lakes. The Great Lakes tributaries have a long and illustrious fly fishing tradition; even Ernest Hemingway wrote that the tributary that connects Lake Superior and Lake Huron was "the greatest rainbow [steelhead] fishing in the world."

Why has traditional fly fishing literature slighted Great Lakes fly fishing for salmon and steelhead? One major reason is that Great Lakes fly anglers use non-traditional techniques and flies. When Great Lakes fly fishing for steelhead is written about in periodicals or books, the presentation is frequently incomplete.

The intent of this book is to be neither traditional nor non-traditional, but to be *truthful*. The focus here is to give the reader an accurate and vivid picture of what has and is really happening in Great Lakes fly fishing. Herein we will allow readers to assess the Great Lakes techniques using their own criteria.

The goal of this volume is not to protect nor bash any fly fishing traditions or attitudes. Nor is it to present purist fly fishing. The object is to paint a real picture of how Great Lakes fly fishermen pursue salmon and steelhead. Much like Horace Walpole, the English author who told his portrait artist to "leave the warts on." Artists and writers that paint the best profile of a subject can often miss the real treasure of the topic or person. Walpole knew that pretty or not, his warts were an intricate part of his features. Personally, I don't consider any of the Great Lakes fly fishing techniques "warts." They are distinctive and colorful threads of the tapestry that portray Midwestern steelhead and salmon fly fishing.

This is not a where-to book about finding that secret nook where you can land a 20-pound plus steelhead—though that is included. This

1

is a how-to book that shares not only how anglers cast flies to these huge migrants but also *why* they cast them. An old Missionary's motto says, "Give a man a fish and you have fed him for a day. *Teach* him to fish and you've fed him for a lifetime." I paraphrase it, "Show a fisherman a good pool, he has good fishing for a day—if someone else doesn't beat him there. But teach him how to find a good pool, and he has great fishing for a lifetime."

> *The real motive of this volume is to give the reader greater understanding, pleasure and success while pursuing these trophy fish*

Herein, you will learn not only how to find a good pool, redd and run, but how to select the best flies, how to cast them into the fish's strike zone, how to locate fish during their migration, and a great deal more.

One goal here is to share a true picture about Great Lakes fly fishing for salmon and steelhead. However, the real motive of this volume is to give the reader greater understanding, pleasure and success while pursuing these trophy fish.

Because of its honesty and completeness, this book represents a benchmark in the evolution of fly fishing in Great Lakes tributaries. I assume no authority to write this guide except that I too have struggled, failed, and even at times succeeded in fooling salmon and steelhead into striking flies I tied. I am just a fellow sojourner and will share my mistakes—falling in, bad casts, getting skunked (no magazine editor gives writing contracts to write about skunked days)—as well as a few successes.

Passion and Pursuit

I often wonder why we have great passion for pursuing these brutes on such light tackle. Maybe the child in me wants to believe that

there are still things in life that man cannot control with all his talents and technology. I want to believe there is still some mystery in the world. I want to feel the unrestrainable surge of a steelhead that strips the line from my hardy reel as easily as a hawk takes flight. I want to attempt an impossible task and at times achieve it.

As a boy, I read *The Golden Hawks of Ghengis Khan* and dreamed of training a hawk to hunt. I dreamed of releasing a trained, wild hawk and watching it return to me on request. Years later, I realized that dream and have caught quarry in almost every region of this nation. But the mystery remains: Why does a hawk that could fly anywhere *choose* to return to me?

Hunting with a 12-gauge shotgun would be more efficient, productive and deadly, just as other methods of fishing can be to fly fishing. But a hawk dancing on the wrist still fascinates me more than a 12-gauge resting on my shoulder. Nor does watching a bobber compare to casting to a rising Brown or Brookie.

Hawks capture quarry four to six times their own weight, so for me the mysterious link between fly fishing and falconry is that neither is the easiest method of pursuing the intended prey. But they may be the most majestic.

This is the first book to fully cover many aspects of Great Lakes fly fishing for salmon and steelhead, including:

- **Drift-fly-fishing with nymph flies for steelhead** also called deep-nymphing. This technique works equally well outside the Great Lakes tributaries, such as for the 20-pound Brown trout of Arkansas' White River, the Northwestern steelhead, Alaskan steelhead, and the Maritime Provinces' Atlantic Salmon
- **"reflex strikes"** by steelhead that take drifting natural nymphs with almost Pavlovian impulse response
- **feeding steelhead** that return to smoult type feeding behavior

🕷 **attitudes of migrant fish**—which include "happy," "feeding" and "stale"

🕷 **passive-aggressive fly fishing technique** to get strikes from "stale" fish

🕷 **fly fishing for the Great Lakes Skamania steelhead** this aspect of the Great Lakes flyfishing could improve the most dramatically this decade

🕷 **catching huge Chinook salmon and spunky Pink salmon on nymph patterns** such as Number 10 Green Caddis Larva

🕷 **tying simple, seductive steelhead and salmon flies**

The last chapter describes many easy-to-tie seductive flies including Egg Cluster flies, Glo Bugs, Green Caddis Larva, Bunny Leeches, 'arrow-Nymphs, and Stonefly Nymph patterns.

The fly fishing traditionalist or purist may not always think that Great Lakes fly fishing techniques are pretty, but no one can slander their effectiveness.

So ready or not here we come, "warts" and all!

Hexegenia Navatalovia **fly—
a "female Hex-nymph on steroids"**

Hen steelhead caught on a fly

The Great Lakes Fly Fishing Evolution

The genesis of fly fishing Great Lakes tributaries
for salmon and steelhead

"What fly are you using?" asked a frustrated fisherman from Wisconsin as he watched me lift a 12-pound steelhead by the tail from a Michigan river.

"Number 10 Green Caddis Larva," I said.

This was the fifth steelhead he and his friend had seen me land in the last hour. I fought each fish downriver and tailed it in some slack water near them, then I'd disappear up around the bend only to reappear with yet another steelhead. They were using the ultra-bright Neon Wiggler pattern with no success. This Neon Wiggler was a Spring Wiggler tied with a neon red body and a chartreuse hackle, wing and tail.

"Do you have any green Caddis flies?"

"No," they said.

"How about Number 10 Black Stone nymphs?"

"No."

"I'll give you some after I release this fish," I said. "The green Caddis and Black Stones are working the best today. There's no magic to it. It's just a matter of matching the natural nymphs and drifting the flies in the steelhead's strike zone."

Moments later I felt the strength of the steelhead return as I held him in the current. As I lowered my hand from under him, he swung his wide tail to catch his balance. His tail pulsed again and he flowed out into the current, gaining speed with each swipe of his tail. We all watched his seemingly effortless knifing through the current toward the deeper run near the opposite bank.

Wading to the near bank I opened my fly box and gave some flies to each of the fishermen.

"These look like trout flies, not steelhead flies," said the older fisherman, a college professor from Wisconsin, as he tied on a Caddis Larva and Stonefly nymph in tandem 24-inches apart.

"They *are* trout flies," I replied, "We just tie them on tougher hooks. They are both Number 10 patterns tied on a Number 8 short-shank hook. I like the bigger gap and larger eye of the Number 8 hooks. The larger eye lets me tie the dropper fly in-line, with two knots in that one eye."

I ran my fingers over my tippet and checked for any nicks or abrasions. This time it was fine.

"Why don't you come up and fish where I was," I suggested. "I have appointments this afternoon and have to leave quickly, but there are still several steelhead up there."

"Sure, that would be great," he said.

As we walked up the bank we both saw the fish holding in the clear, shallow water of the redd. Slowly he eased into position across and upstream of the fish.

Hex-nymph, Green Caddis Larva, Black Stonefly Nymph, Neon Wiggler

"Cast about fourteen feet upstream of the fish," I suggested. "If your fly line pauses when the flies pass through the fish—*set the hook*! They're taking very lightly today."

On his third cast, he hooked a 10-pound hen. She took the green Caddis. When he set the hook, she bolted away from him and immediately his

reel began to sing. He waded out into a shallow run and as she turned downriver he waded down with her. She fought toward some logs but he turned her back and soon we were downriver at the same sandy, slack water where I had landed the previous five fish. I tailed her for him.

He was amazed.

I was too.

How could a knowledgeable fly fisherman who traveled so far for steelhead know nothing about nymphing for steelhead? The answer in part is the vast difference between Northwest techniques—which get all the press—and Great Lakes techniques. If anglers bring Northwestern techniques to Great Lakes tributaries, the confusion can become great, like it did for these avid fly fishermen. Their predicament is not uncommon.

Until recently, for instance, the sets of steelhead flies sold in the fly fishing catalogs completely misrepresented the flies typically used in Great Lakes tributaries. The flies used to catch 90% of Great Lakes steelhead were not even displayed, much less sold. Recently while in a fly shop, a fly fishing guide showed me a new steelheading book with a complete page listing over twenty different "Great Lakes steelhead patterns." He then asked me how many of those flies were in my fly boxes—we were going fishing the next morning. I said, "Only one. Maybe."

He replied that he had only two! It was a Northwest steelheading book. No wonder there is such confusion.

The Western patterns do work here in the Midwest on steelhead with the *same attitude* as the fish they pursue out West. As we will see later, the number of fish with *that* attitude is often the smallest percentage of the fish in a river. Therefore Great Lakes fly fishermen developed different flies—nymphs especially— to seduce a higher percentage of the fish in the river to strike a fly.

> *Understanding the stream variants will increase your success in each season of the migration.*

Recently, the fly fishing catalogs have begun selling steelhead fly sets that include the flies popular with Great Lakes fly anglers. In part, this is because of the increasing popularity of steelhead and salmon in Great Lakes tributaries. The number of anglers who now travel here to fish has grown and includes authors, editors, and those in the fly fishing industry. Yet success is not as easy as just buying the correct flies.

Determining Factors For
Migrant Strikes

Buying or tying the right steelhead and salmon flies is only one factor that an angler must understand to be consistently successful at hooking these huge river migrants.

Any one moment on the river is the culmination of many different components flowing together into that angling experience. Every angler realizes that at times we are at the unpredictable whim of the weather. A cold snap in late March that drives the water temperature down a few degrees can radically upset your week-long fishing vacation. Other times you arrive on the river when a warm spring storm is approaching. It's overcast, warm—even muggy—and the steelhead take flies aggressively like smallmouth protecting their spawning beds. The fishing is incredible. *That* was

the fortunate situation I found myself in the morning I landed the 12-pound steelhead and spoke with the Wisconsin professor.

We are also at the whim of a multitude of factors that all converge like feeder streams trickling and uniting until they become the "river of time" we fish on any one day. Understanding these "feeder stream" factors allows you to best determine which flies, fly fishing techniques, and river locations will yield the highest percentage of strikes from steelhead or salmon that day.

Why will a steelhead strike? Or, maybe better, why doesn't a steelhead strike?

The "feeder stream" factors determine why and if migrating steelhead and salmon strike flies—or any other lure or bait for that matter. Understanding and considering these variants will increase your success in each season of the migration. These variants include:

- the water temperature
- the water temperature relative to yesterday's water temperature
- the stage of the fish's migration
- current flow through that particular stretch of river; such as deep run, deep pool, cluttered pool, deep-water redd, shallow redd, shallow run, undercut bank . . . Each of these has its own set of factors
- the attitude of the pod of fish; are they happy, feeding or stale?
- water clarity
- current speed
- the "emotional state" of the fish; harassed, spawning, aggressive, fighting
- the *direction* of the barometric pressure
- the sulunar calendar; indication when the "bite" is most likely to occur
- aquatic insect activity; Stone flies hatching? *Hexagenia* nymphs free drifting? Spawning fish dislodging Caddis?
- does this area of the river have any natural food traps, such as an eddy that collects free drifting eggs?

color of the fly; there are dozens of choices including green olive (Caddis Larva flies alone offer a dozen shades and colors to choose), chartreuse, black, brown, tan, cream, rust, yellow, red, and every Glo-Bugs® yarn color for egg patterns.

size of fly; too large a fly can spook fish even if it represents the correct color and species

leader length changes with the depth of the current, stretch of river, brightness of light and clarity of water

diameter of tippet; thinner *always* results in more fish hooked but not landed

position to stand while casting

which fly fishing technique will be the most effective; floating line with strike indicator? Sinktip or shootinghead? Drift-fly-fishing with a Slinky Drifter?

where to cast to get the flies in fish's strike zone

how to get the longest drag-free drift

when to swing streamers through runs to find the fish

That is at least thirty-six variants and sub-factors and it is just a *partial* list to give us the idea of the complexity of the variables. *See chart on facing page.*

"A Fishing Moment"

These are some factors that affect any particular moment on the river. The change in any one of these items can affect a change in your fly, tippet or technique that you will use. It may also require a change in the nook that you decide to fish, which stretch of river, or even which river system you choose.

The change in one of these factors, no matter how remote it may seem from the "fishing moment," can produce a dramatic change in the fishing conditions. That change could necessitate a different fishing technique, size of tippet and kind of fly. A change at the top of

the chart can affect a change in the whole *stream of consciousness* of that river moment. If one factor changes the rest can topple like dominoes.

> *The change in one of these factors, no matter how remote it may seem from the "fishing moment," can produce a dramatic change in the fishing conditions.*

If, for instance, the water clarity changes from clear to dark, this can affect *everything*. If the water temperature changes, the clarity usually changes as well. If the water is dark because of spring runoff, the water temperature will be dropping. If the causative factor is a warm fall—or even spring—rain, the water temperature can rise. This dark water will then affect the stage of migration—bringing fish into the rivers if it is fall, and pushing fish into deep pools if it is the spring runoff.

Solutions

As each chapter unfolds, the implication of and solutions to these various factors will be discussed for each season of the steelhead migration and for each salmon species. For now let's preface and clarify what some of these factors imply.

Attitude: The attitude of a pod of migrating salmon or steelhead greatly determines if they are inclined to strike a fly, and what kind of fly they will pursue. As we will see in Chapter Two, migrating salmon and steelhead can possess three different attitudes—"Happy," "Feeding" or "Stale." A Happy fish makes any angler who encounters it happy. Happy fish are the carefree, aggressive, playful fish that strike just for the sheer pleasure of exploring the unknown. A Feeding fish takes flies that imitate natural food items occurring in the river that day—such as nymphs and eggs. However, we

Contributing Factors that Produce "A Fishing Moment"

Clear
Clouded
Dark   Clarity
         Water
Increasing   Temperature
Decreasing

Down-pour
Sprinkling
    Raining
    Overcast
    Snowing
    Sunny
Barometric Pressure
Direction of air temperature
    Sunlunar Indicators
         Weather Conditions

Happy
Feeding
    Stale
    Attitudes of Fish

Sink tip
    Strike indicator
    Shooting-head
    Drift fly-fishing
         Technique

Harassed
Spawning
    Aggressive
         Emotional State of Fish

                        Summer
                    Fall
                    Winter
Stage of   Spring
Migration

                Insects uprooted
                from spawning gravel
                Hatching Flies
                Free drifting nymphs
                Free drifting eggs
Aquatic Insects

                        Fast run
                        Fast redd
                        Slow run
                        Confluence
                        Cluttered pool
                        Long slow pool
                        Undercut bank
                        Shallow run
                        Shallow redd
                        Shallow pool
                        Deep run
                        Deep pool
                        Deep water redd
                Speed
Current Flow   Depth

                        Type
                    Color
                    Size
Fly

                    Tippet length
                    Tippet diameter
                    Tippet color
Leader

encounter Stale fish more often than Happy or Feeding fish. Migrant fish adopt this stale attitude because they have been harassed by heavy fishing pressure, stung by hooks, spooked by anglers, or have become completely intent on spawning. These fish are the hardest to get to strike a fly. Yet, as we shall see, it can be done effectively and continuously.

> *When hot weather increases the water temperatures, the summer run steelhead seek the coolest water in the stream*

Season: The season of the steelhead's migration is also an important factor. A steelhead in the river in summer will strike a fly for different reasons than a fish in the river during the spring spawning time. Fall has its unique traits too, including the location of the steelhead and the influence of the salmon run. Winter has its own chilling set of requirements for success. Spring blossoms with the expectation of success—it has the most fish to chase—but they are the fish most reluctant to seduction.

Water Temperature: Water temperature is often a huge contributor to the fly fishing success and strategy. The *direction* the water temperature is moving also greatly affects the fish. For instance, in the winter, if the water temperature rises a couple of degrees in late afternoon, that is the best time for fishing. In the winter season the water temperatures become *the* most important factor for fishing success. In the summer, the water can actually become too hot for the summer run steelhead, just as it is too hot for the trout. An increase in the water temperature on those summer afternoons will shut off any chance of a strike unless you know where to find the coolest water in the river. The summer steelhead will surely find it.

Barometric Pressure: The barometric pressure affects salmon and steelhead in much that same way it affects other fish—and even people. A shifting barometric pressure will affect the *degree* to which salmon and steelhead will bite. I hate it when I arrive at the river only to realize that the wind is out of the East. Remember the old rhyme that ends, "Wind out of the East, fish bite least!" Conversely, one of my favorite times to fish for steelhead is the two hours before a warm spring rainstorm.

Water Clarity: The clarity of the current flow will influence the kind, size and color of the flies you use. If the water is high and dark—"chocolate milk"—and you are using the same size 8 and 10 nymphs that were successful for spawning fish in clear water, you will have a long day. However, if you use large Number 4 or 2 streamers, in colors bright enough to spook a whole pod of fish in clear water, you increase your chances of success by several fold. Water clarity also influences the size of the tippet you can use while still soliciting the maximum number of strikes.

> *Migrating salmon and steelhead can possess three different attitudes—Happy, Feeding or Stale*

Sulunar Calendar: Many national outdoor magazines publish Sulunar calendars showing the best time *on that particular day* for the fish to be "on the bite." Jim Teeny told me that there is usually a certain time for each day when the steelhead go "on the bite." My experience of living a mile from a quality fly fishing river and fishing almost daily according to the Sulunar calendar confirms that the fish are the most active *on that day* during the Sulunar time given.

Feeding: The presence of natural food items that the fish see all day long determines what fly to cast. Imitating the most abundant food source increases the number of strikes. But as we will see, it is not as simple as, "Well, it's spawning time, so let's cast yarn eggs all day."

Spawning With Opportunities

In the Great Lakes region we are blessed with vast year-round opportunities for salmon and steelhead fishing. Without being an excellent angler, I have caught steelhead in every month of the year on flies from Great Lakes tributaries. The fly angler can enjoy a long and productive steelhead season by fishing the spring runs in March in the southern range of the Great Lakes—Indiana, Ohio, New York, Wisconsin and the southern tributaries of Michigan and the Province of Ontario (see the chart on page 13 that shows the weather zones of the Great Lake Tributaries). Then, as the weather and the rivers warm up, the angler can fish the major runs of favorite rivers. On the rivers with strong natural runs there is some good steelhead fishing in May and even into early June. The rivers in May and June also have less steelhead fishing pressure.

April and May also opens up fishing further north. Fishing the upper sections of the Great Lakes, especially the tributaries of Lake Superior and the St. Mary's Rapids—a tributary of Lake Huron and the natural "spill-way" of Lake Superior—can provide excellent steelhead fishing through May and into late June.

July and August bring the summer run steelhead into the rivers. As we will see later, the strongest runs are in Indiana's small creeks, but many other rivers are blossoming with their own strong runs—Michigan's St. Joe River and the Big Manistee River in particular. The Atlantic salmon begin running selected rivers beginning in July and August and continue into November.

August, September and October bring a rush of salmon into the rivers—Kings and Pinks first, then later the Coho salmon follow. Fall steelhead follow these salmon but they often get lost in the salmon's mad rush, until October and November when the largest fall steelhead runs enter the rivers. December brings steelheading as a gift to those who find time amid the Holiday celebrations.

If January provides warm enough days and you catch the water temperatures rising, winter will surrender some shining steelhead that glisten brighter than the sun off the snow. As winter wrenches itself free from February's grip and spring peers around the corner, some summer run steelhead use any slight rise in the frigid water temperatures to start spawning. Most of the spring spawning steelhead migrate into the rivers as the late winter run-off and spring rains swell the rivers. These Happy fish are greeted with glee by the anglers longing for fish to take the flies they tied on those long cold winter nights.

> *In the Great Lakes we are blessed with vast year-round opportunities for salmon and steelhead fishing*

Then the annual cycle of spring spawning begins again in March and I'm ready to go along for the ride. In the past, each year added another "quest" to my fishing agenda, like landing a "Master Angler" steelhead on a fly; catching steelhead on a traditional Atlantic salmon fly and a Spey fly; catching Pink salmon on a fly; tailing a Coho salmon; landing Atlantic salmon on traditional "full-dressed" streamers and on nymphs; and catching an Atlantic and a steelhead on a dry fly.

One joy of living in the Great Lakes region is having all these trophy fly fishing opportunities in our backyard—ah, our neighboring rivers and streams. It's a small wonder that anglers journey from all over the United States and parts of Canada to fly fish the Great Lakes tributaries.

But when they get here they are often surprised by both the number and accessibility of the fish and the techniques and flies we use.

The Midwestern Fly Fishing Evolution from traditional streamers to nymphs and naturals

Over the last twenty-five years, the Great Lakes flies for steelhead and salmon have evolved from the traditional Northwest streamers to nymphs and naturals. The journey was a natural one, spurred on by ever-increasing angling pressure on the fishery and the ambition to catch not only the happy and feeding fish, but also the stale fish. The stale fish are the most reluctant fish to strike a fly.

The Great Lakes angler's journey from traditional steelhead flies to nymphs is illustrated by Bob Nicholson's personal fly fishing journey. Nicholson began guiding on Lake Michigan tributaries when guiding was almost unknown in the Midwest. He currently lives and guides out of the Baldwin Creek Motel, which

Bob Nicholson

he owns and operates with his wife, Chris. In the mid-1980s he moved permanently to Baldwin, Michigan from the Detroit area.

"I began fly fishing for steelhead up here twenty-five years ago, because I encountered a dentist in a sporting goods store in late February," Nicholson explained, describing his own migration. "This dentist was looking to buy a sinking fly line. Because he was in such a rush to own one, I asked him what he was going to do with it. He said he was going fishing the next weekend to the Pere Marquette river for steelhead. I was startled.

"Over the years I had often fished for steelhead but never on a fly. I had been wet-fly fishing since I was a little boy, but didn't know you could catch steelhead on a fly rod. So the next weekend I went up to the Pere Marquette.

"That weekend in early March there were 12 to 14 inches of snow, and I came up with a buddy who was not a fly fisherman. We walked around like pilgrims. I encountered two other anglers, a father and a son, and they taught me how to catch steelhead. The technique then was to tease the fish with a fly like a Royal Coachman bucktail. The father told me, 'If you come down here tomorrow morning and fish in this spot, you'll catch a fish.' And I did! I used the technique he showed me. Landing that one fish got me hooked."

When Nicholson fished there in the early 1970s, there would only be six or eight cars in the parking lot at the High Banks at the peak of the season. He said he would be really irritated if it was that crowded. If he came up on a weekday and saw two or three anglers the whole day, *that* would be a crowd. So his knowledge of fly fishing was all self-taught. By the time Nicholson permanently moved up north in 1984, the rivers were busy at peak times but few river guides existed—maybe three or four others. For his first couple of years, Nicholson guided from a canoe and only on the "flies-

Zones of the Great Lakes Tributaries

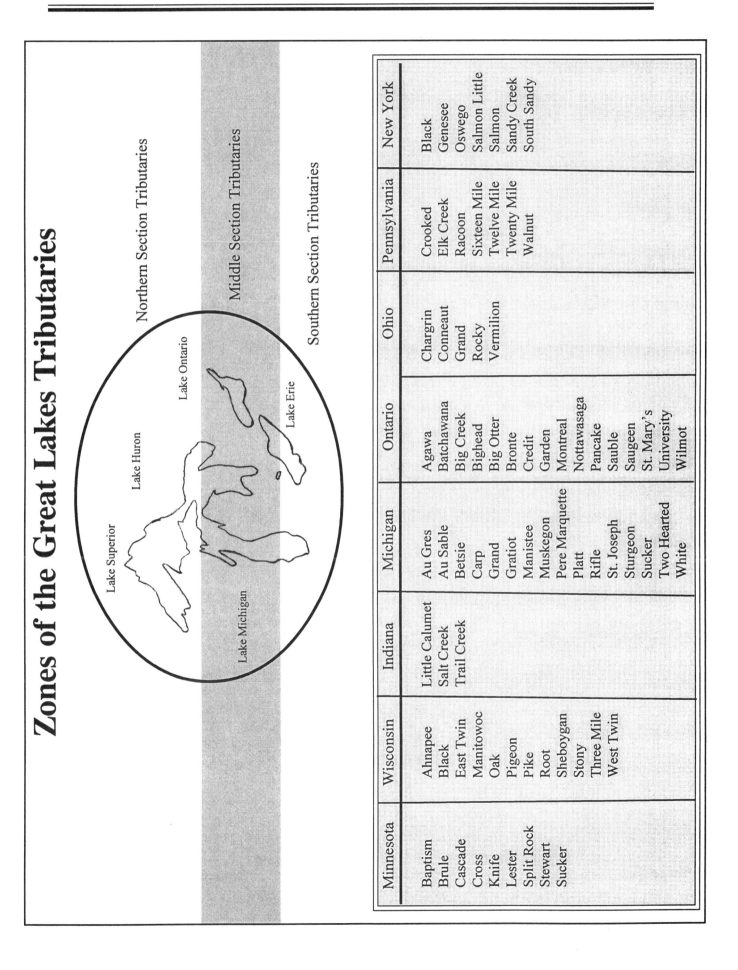

Northern Section Tributaries

Middle Section Tributaries

Southern Section Tributaries

Minnesota	Wisconsin	Indiana	Michigan	Ontario	Ohio	Pennsylvania	New York
Baptism	Ahnapee	Little Calumet	Au Gres	Agawa	Chargrin	Crooked	Black
Brule	Black	Salt Creek	Au Sable	Batchawana	Conneaut	Elk Creek	Genesee
Cascade	East Twin	Trail Creek	Betsie	Big Creek	Grand	Racoon	Oswego
Cross	Manitowoc		Carp	Bighead	Rocky	Sixteen Mile	Salmon Little
Knife	Oak		Grand	Big Otter	Vermilion	Twelve Mile	Salmon
Lester	Pigeon		Gratiot	Bronte		Twenty Mile	Sandy Creek
Split Rock	Pike		Manistee	Credit		Walnut	South Sandy
Stewart	Root		Muskegon	Garden			
Sucker	Sheboygan		Pere Marquette	Montreal			
	Stony		Platt	Nottawasaga			
	Three Mile		Rifle	Pancake			
	West Twin		St. Joseph	Sauble			
			Sturgeon	Saugeen			
			Sucker	St. Mary's			
			Two Hearted	University			
			White	Wilmot			

only" water of the Pere Marquette. Later he bought a driftboat. In those years they were never bothered by crowds. And the anglers that came "fished the river."

"We'd fish point 'A,' then we moved to point 'B,' then point 'C'." Nicholson reflects. "At that time there were four or five driftboats on the river. When they passed you they would say, 'I'll give you the next three bends.' And we would fish the river. Things are different now.

"For me, the evolution from streamers to nymphs began sometime in the 1970s when I ran into Ron Spring on the river," Nicholson

Spring Wiggler

continued. "Ron came into a run that I had been banging away on with bucktail streamers. I had fished my heart out there for a couple hours. Ron waded downriver and with three casts into this dark run, he hooked a fish. In thirty minutes he caught three fish. I thought, *This isn't right, I have been here for hours and he comes in here like he does this all the time*. Remember, though, in those years, the river wasn't crowded, so these fish weren't all uptight or harassed.

"'What fly are you using?' I asked.

"'My fly.' Ron said.

"'Well, show it to me,' I said.

"He wouldn't give me one, so I memorized

it and went home to tie some 'Spring Wigglers' in several colors. This Spring Wiggler is like a Woolly Worm with squirrel tail tied in for a tail and pulled over the top to the eye.

"On a later day, I saw Ron and his younger brother on the river. Ron was fishing with his Shakespeare 1810 reel when he hooked a fish. While he fought the fish the reel blew up. His younger brother said something about 'that stupid reel.' But Ron said, 'This reel doesn't owe me anything, that's the 63rd fish this season.' The Spring Wiggler is a great fly."

Nicholson said he started using Ron's Wiggler pattern and caught more fish. That began his progression away from teasing fish with streamers. It then began a natural genesis toward trying other nymphs like a Number 6 Hare's Ear nymph, then to other sizes and patterns. As the fishing pressure built over the years, Nicholson and other anglers began looking for ways to catch spooked fish.

"I remember tying a scud on a Mustad #2457 hook because it had a decent gap on a Number 12," Nicholson said. "I tied a Hare's Ear nymph on it too. One night I thought, *No ten pound fish will ever take that fly*. Then the next day we caught fish—including a ten pounder—when no one else was catching anything. Then I thought, *Let's try that in olive and black*. At that time we were concerned more with colors and sizes than fly patterns.

"Then in the middle 1980s came the Glo Bug revolution. That changed everything. Fisherman came back from Alaska with Glo Bugs that had been so successful. We soon learned that the yarn flies worked great in the Midwest, too. There even was a time when I fished a

'Stop-Light rig' for salmon and fall steelhead. For weeks I didn't use nymphs at all. This rig had a green fly on the bottom and a red one on the dropper—a stoplight. In those years we had many more fish.

> *The goal is to select a fly that can attract a strike from all three types of fish that are in the river*

"Now I fish with a combination of several nymphs, several colored Glo Bugs and some streamers," Nicholson concluded. "I now consider the Spring Wiggler more of a streamer pattern than a nymph, but it was the fly that pushed us toward using more natural flies. Especially as the fishing pressure became more intense and we were trying to get stale or harassed fish to strike."

The Evolution of Great Lakes Fly Fishing Techniques

Bob Nicholson also experienced an evolution of fly fishing techniques simultaneous to his fly evolution. His journey was joined by hundreds of thousands of anglers over those decades. Nicholson explains:

"In 1972 or 1973, I ran into a guy who was fishing spring steelhead. He said, 'Hey, you should come in the fall and fish for salmon, they are a lot of fun and they'll hit big streamers.'

"I had been messing around with the salmon, they were new . . . I came up that fall with my wife for the weekend, to get away from the kids. We parked the camper at the High Banks on the Pere Marquette. Our's was the only vehicle there. We walked down to the Deer Lick and to my astonishment in front of me were between 50 and 100 salmon. Salmon paved the bottom of the river. I had my 8-weight rod, and had read some articles about catching salmon on the Smith River out west. I had tied some Comet style flies, in case I would run into some

of these salmon. I had gotten some waders for my wife, and asked her if she wanted to fish for these. She said, 'No, they're too big! But I'll watch.'

"So I fished for them," Nicholson continued. "I started to cast and I hooked them in the back. You could hardly get the flies through the run without hitting one of them. I was using a floating line with a tapered leader with the Comet fly. I was having a hard time getting down into the fish, though the Deer Lick section of the Pere Marquette is not very deep. So I put on a couple of split-shot a foot or so ahead of the fly. Then I still hooked them in the tail, or the back, and I would just hold on and soon the hook would pull out. I cast for forty-two minutes and foul-hooked lots of fish, too many really. Finally after forty-two minutes a salmon bit the fly, and well, you talk about a time!

"There we were, hooked to this fish," Nicholson said, grinning widely. "What were we to do? There was a hunter down at the Chap's cabin and he saw this fish thrashing around, and I only had this small woman to help me. He knew we had a problem. He came running up the river with a little $5 aluminum trout net and asked to help. I said, 'No, thank you.'

> *Great Lakes flies for steelhead and salmon have evolved from the traditional Northwest streamers to nymphs and naturals*

"Well, I wound up landing the fish and it was a Coho about nine or ten pounds. I thought that was terrific and it made my day; we had gotten the job done and caught a salmon on a fly. We went out and ate dinner. Then later we got into larger salmon, and I went home and told a couple friends. When we came back, we still had a terrible time getting the salmon to bite.

"I remember the following year I made several trips up here, without a fly rod, to walk the river just looking for fish. I checked down below Bowman Bridge, because I had heard that the steelhead would come up and stay. Then I began playing with tackle, and it became obvious in 1975 that you needed to use some lead to get the flies down. We were using lead on the line for steelhead. Many fishermen used spinning gear with flies on the 'flies-only' water.

"It was while salmon fishing to visible fish and casting to them repeatedly that I decided to use split-shot. I bought some inexpensive 4-weight level line and used some stout leader, then tied some exotic knots to get from the heavy butt section to the tippet section. Somewhere in the 1970s the light turned on and I took my drift-fishing background and tied on a barrel swivel. With that swivel I only needed to tie one knot, not several exotic knots to get from the heavy butt section to the tippet. I used a Uni-knot to tie the butt section to the fly line, then tied a barrel swivel at the other end. I then attached the small tippet with a 20-pound butt section above. The swivel becomes a mechanical device to simplify the fishing. On my leader I always use a rod length—at least nine feet—and you have very little fly line in the water. If you show a fish the fly line you will spook a fish, I don't care what people say. But not so with mono down there.

"For a year Ray Schmidt called me a 'fat line fisherman,' because I resisted using a shooting fly line. My style of fishing is to follow the fly, like nymphing with flies. Mend and mend and get the fly-line behind the flies and follow them. I finally went to the shooting line on a professional level, because my nymphing technique was too difficult to teach a novice. Nowadays, I teach drift-fly-fishing technique with a dropper fly and a point fly.

"For trout I still fish classic wet flies; I take great pride in tying these old fashioned flies. I learned to fly fish by reading Ray Burdman's books. The adult fly fishermen I knew as a boy were all wet fly fishermen, with a hand twist retrieve. The dropper fly was not foreign to me. For years I didn't think I was fishing unless I had three flies on the end of my fly line."

The last twenty-five years have proved that the Great Lakes fly fishermen are more likely to experiment with different flies and techniques to increase success. They are less inhibited about breaking tradition. This has allowed for the many fly fishing innovations of the Great Lakes. But it has not changed the passion with which Great Lakes fly anglers pursue this sport. Nor does it suppress the frustration when we cannot tempt a salmon or steelhead to strike.

Understanding *why* and when they strike and will lead you to greater fishing success and more fun. That leads us to the next chapter— *Why* Salmon and Steelhead Strike Flies.

Pink Salmon

Strikes from Salmon and Steelhead
The Flies and the Whys

Few fishing topics spark more questions than, "Why do migrating steelhead and salmon strike flies?" Far too often the question and answers are too simplistic. For sure, there is not one "super, catch-all, fail-proof fly."

John Hunter, my friend and a fly fishing guide, was fishing the fall Chinook salmon run, and had tied up a purple Matuka streamer for the occasion. After fishing most of the day with very few strikes, he moved to a new pool that held a pod of salmon. He decided to try the purple Matuka. *What do I have to lose?* He thought. He then proceeded to hook a dozen fish before he lost the fly on a very fresh, huge Chinook. Later he told me that he thought he had found the "perfect salmon fly." That night he stayed up late and tied two dozen purple Matuka streamers.

The following day he fished over several pods of salmon and the purple never got a strike. Hunter later realized that "the purple salmon killer" was so successful that first day because he had encountered a pod of fresh, happy fish that would strike *any* fly. That realization came only after wasting hours tying and fishing with a good but not wonderful fly. He realized his mistake was not fully understanding *why* that pod of salmon had taken the purple Matuka.

Jim Johnson, a fly fishing guide and co-owner of Johnson's Pere Marquette Lodge in Baldwin, Michigan, said, "I stress the importance of understanding why various steelhead or salmon strike at a particular time. Fish in fresh from the lake will hit a fly for much different reasons than spawning fish. For instance, fish will hit much differently in warm water temperatures than in cold water temperatures.

"There are three reasons why steelhead strike a fly: first is they're feeding, second is they're protecting their territory, and third is they're just *playing*. By 'playing' I mean like a cat plays with yarn that you dance across the floor. If you know why a fish took your fly last time, it will be easier to repeat it next time.

"Many people get confused with this concept in all kinds of fishing" Johnson continued. "If, for instance, you're trout fishing and you throw a fly that doesn't resemble any natural food on the water and the fish takes the fly, you could mistakenly think you have found a good imitation for what is hatching. In fact, the fish didn't take that for food at all, it took the fly because that fish was in a playful mood and experimented by feeling the fly with its mouth."

Attitudes of Migrant Fish

Before you can know what flies to cast to fish, you must understand the *attitude* of those fish. Are they fresh, active, aggressive and playful—"happy" fish? Are they actively feeding fish? Are they spawning? Or are they stale fish, those reluctant and skittish fish that resist provocation? Migratory fish fit into one of these three attitude categories:

- **Happy fish**—fresh, active, playful, or aggressive
- **Feeding fish**—actively eating the natural food in the river
- **Stale fish**—skittish, shy, reluctant, harassed or spawning.

Determining the attitude of your target fish greatly influences what flies you cast. As we will see in Chapter Three, it will also decide which fly fishing technique will be the most successful. The fish's attitude and the river conditions—which are intimately intertwined—determine "a successful fly" on any particular day. Misunderstanding these factors can lead to errant views and long days on the river. You cannot just cast small nymphs in every season, into every run, pool and redd, expecting optimum success, or a triumphant day. So much depends on the fish's attitude, but every angler loves to encounter happy fish.

Happy fish

Happy fish are the least reluctant of any fish you will ever encounter. They strike flies just for the fun of it. They will charge to the surface and grab a gurgling Bomber fly just to touch it with their mouths. Unfortunately, happy fish are regularly the minority of the fish in the river, because many factors can sour their happy attitude.

Happiness is an emotion based on what is *happen*ing around us—our circumstances. Happiness comes from the Scottish word, "happenstance." If the circumstances around you are positive, then you will be happy. If a migrant fish is surrounded by positive circumstances, it too will be happy. If a salmon or steelhead has shelter from the current, feels protected from predators (including anglers), is well fed, and swims in water not too cold or too warm, this content and stress-free fish will be happy. A pod of happy fish can migrate into the river together, especially in September for salmon and late March for steelhead. These fish are full of energy from their years in the big lake, comfortable water temperatures lured them into the river, and they have not been heavily fished or stung by hooks . . . yet.

> *Before you can know what flies to cast to fish, you must understand the attitude of those fish*

These happy fish are stress-free and looking to experiment and touch every new, exciting thing in the river. Nymphs, minnows, and even hatching flies are not beyond their area of pursuit. Happy fish will swim across the river, even through heavy current, to investigate a bomber fly chugging across the surface. They strike flies no self-respecting trout would ever touch. They waste energy chasing quarry that, if caught, would not begin to repay the energy expended to catch it. But the happy fish doesn't care. Why should it? It doesn't have a care in the world. After all, life is carefree and stress-free. Why not relax? They are like college students whose parents pay all their bills, they just want to have fun.

Sadly, for both the students and steelhead, their carefree and stress-free lifestyle ends much too abruptly. The stress of being fished and hooked soon sours their happy attitude. However, if you find a pod of happy steelhead or salmon, you will never forget them. Nor will you stop pursuing them. Encountering happy fish makes up for every fishless, biteless day you'll ever spend on the river.

The Happiest Fish

Pink salmon are the happiest fish I know. My father-in-law, Vic Bierschbach, and I were on our last fishing trip together before his death from cancer. While he rested in the motorhome, I walked into a Pink salmon river. Standing on one rock over a wide run, I caught and released one Pink salmon after another. The night before, I had stayed up late tying flies while listening to a Canadian Country Western station. Maybe it was the sad lyrics, or the rhythm and blues that motivated me, but I tied several weird patterns after I had finished my standard salmon flies. One strange fly was an Egg Cluster tied with two powder-blue and two royal-blue Pom-Poms. Another fly was a gaudy streamer with scraps of tinsel, brightly colored bucktail and Krystal flash. Both flies I was sure would *never* catch a fish. After catching so many salmon from that one rock, I experimented with as many different kinds of flies as possible. I tried to find a fly that these salmon would *not* take. After I had caught a salmon on every other type of fly in my box, I tied on the two rejects from my tying-bench wastebasket. This pod of happy salmon decided that even these two flies—that have never caught a fish or solicited a strike in the years since—deserved to get nailed just because they were in the river.

Both flies were taken long after the dead-drift had ended and they were swinging through the tail of the run. Everyone loves to fish for happy fish; they make anglers happy too. These fish do not care what fly or technique you use as long as you get the fly into the river.

Happy fish are the reason so many Western fly fishing books talk about having "no idea why steelhead strike." Happy fish don't need or want a reason to strike a particular fly. Color and size are no real hindrance. All they care about is experiencing or playing with something new.

> *Understanding fish attitudes will lead you to the most effective flies and techniques to catch them*

Happy fish are most often encountered when they first enter the river. They are usually fresh fish that haven't been in the river very long. The Skamania steelhead and summer run Chinook salmon are happy for a longer time because they are in the river waiting for their spawning time to begin. In the summer there are fewer fish in the river but the highest percentage is happy fish. See the chart on page 21 comparing percentages between happy, feeding and stale steelhead for each season of the year. As the fish stay in the river they shift over into "feeding fish." Then finally, as spawning time arrives, they forget all their former playful, happy attitudes. Before spawning season the fish can be soured by encounters with anglers or other stresses. The happy salmon get a stale attitude from anglers or a complete focus on spawning. As fall steelhead "winter-over" in the river and the cold water temperatures put stress on them, they become stale or at best, "feeding fish."

For steelhead that enter the river in the spring, their time as happy fish is shortened. They quickly move into a spawning attitude, which easily makes them so monomaniacal that they become stale fish. If they are in the river a

John Hunter with a 30-pound-plus King Salmon

few weeks before the water temperatures and conditions become suitable for spawning, water temperatures can affect the attitude of happy fish from day to day. For instance, you may encounter a pod of happy fish and that night the water temperature could fall a couple degrees (sometimes as little as one degree). The happy fish then become soured and act like stale fish because of the stress of colder water temperatures.

This happens often in the spring when the water temperatures hover in the low 40s. If the water temperature stabilizes for a couple days and the fish adjust to the colder water, they become more active. These fresh fish quickly become happy again if the water temperature rises. Day to day there are several circumstances—happenstance—that affect the attitude of migrant fish. Understanding them will lead you to the most effective flies and techniques to catch them.

Happy fish will strike big, bright flies if they have not yet been stung or harassed by anglers. Happy fish are the primary fish that the Northwestern fishing techniques and flies target. Once the fish are no longer happy, the

Western anglers call them "stale fish." Usually Northwestern anglers leave these stale fish in pursuit of other happy fish. They also avoid fishing for spawning fish that are most often stale fish.

Feeding Fish

The second most enjoyable migrants to encounter on the river is a pod of feeding fish. A decade ago, many fishermen believed that steelhead and salmon did not feed once they entered the river to spawn. That "fact" many believed, and disbelievers were scorned.

Steelhead and salmon can spend as much as eighteen months in the river as smoult before they journey into one of the Great Lakes to grow into the monsters we encounter on the spawning runs. During their first several months they feed in the river just like the resident trout. They rise to hatching mayflies, stoneflies and caddis. They also gobble up any nymph that passes them. They eat some spring or fall eggs from the spawning fish. When these fish return to the river after their years in the big lake, their subconscious memory of feeding on these nymphs must be reactivated—much like driving through a childhood neighborhood revives memories of experiences and hangouts.

When the migrating salmon and steelhead re-enter the river, they confront a steady parade of nymphs they ate as youngsters. Their automatic temptation is to try them again. Some steelhead even gorge themselves on the nymphs. Others take flies only if they happen to drift directly in front of them.

Seasonal Chart of Steelhead Attitudes

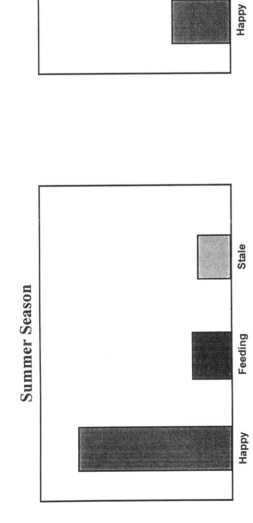

Summer Season

Happy Feeding Stale

The total number of fish in the river may be only 10% of number of steelhead in the Spring Run

Fall Season

Happy Feeding Stale

The total number of fish in the river may be near 25% of number of steelhead in the Spring Run

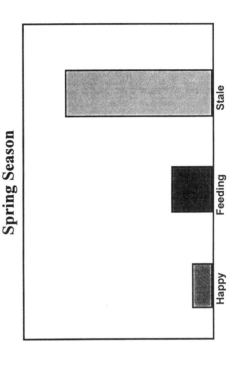

Spring Season

Happy Feeding Stale

The total number of fish in the river is 100% of the number of steelhead in the Spring Run

Winter Season

Happy Feeding Stale

The total number of fish in the river may be near 40% of number of steelhead in the Spring Run

While I was sight fishing steelhead I repeatedly saw a steelhead open its mouth to spit out a fly that it took. Often I was too late at setting the hook. Yet on the following casts I hooked that same fish on the same fly. My experience shows the flies most frequently struck in this behavior are green Caddis larvae flies, stonefly nymphs, (cream colored) latex wigglers, Sparrow nymphs (or 'arrow-Nymphs), and *Hexagenia* nymphs. I have also experienced days when the steelhead focused on only *one* type of insect, such as a Hex-nymph or a stonefly nymph—casting anything else was useless. Sometimes the same is true during salmon spawning runs with Glo Bugs or Egg Cluster flies.

Dick Pobst, the operator of the Thornapple Fly Shop in Ada, Michigan, wrote of his realization of feeding steelhead in his benchmark article in the February, 1991 *Fly Fisherman* magazine. "One April day in the middle of steelhead spawning season, a guy named Dick Smith came into my fly shop. Dick, a fine and knowledgeable fisherman, had spent two seasons in the Pacific Northwest learning how to fish for steelhead, before steelhead fishing became common in Michigan.

"On this particular day the usually laconic Smith was excited. 'I just caught several steelhead on black stonefly nymphs,' he said. 'There was a big emergence of the flies, and the fish were going crazy over them.'

"I commented that this was indeed strange, since steelhead do not feed in the river. 'Sure they do.' Dick said. 'They may not feed as heavily as they do at other stages of life, but they do feed. Today they were going nuts over those nymphs.'

"I grabbed some large black stonefly nymphs and my steelhead flyrod and headed for the river," Pobst wrote. "My most vivid memory of that day was seeing a big male steelhead accelerate off the spawning bed to smack an artificial nymph 10 to 12 feet away. I kept that fish, and when I opened him up, I found the remains of 18 to 20 stonefly nymphs in his stomach. I won't say the fish was in the midst of expelling milt to fertilize eggs, but he was definitely spawning—hogging the redd and driving other males away."

Pobst also enlisted the help of some fly fishing guides who examined the stomachs of each fish that their clients kept. Pobst wrote, "While most reports indicated that steelhead feeding was light and sporadic, some said that the fish actually gorged on certain insects. It was just like trout feeding during a dry-fly hatch, except that the flies were not available as dry flies. When the food was available in great quantities, the fish would feed selectively on the predominant hatch and ignore offerings that were different from their preferred food."

Months	# of Fish	Contents
October	7	Salmon eggs
&	5	Eggs & Caddis
November	5	Caddis Larvae
	15	Empty
	32	
December	3	Caddis Larvae
	7	Empty
	10	
January	0	No Fish Killed
February	7	Tiny Stonefly
&		Nymphs (3 gorged)
March	2	Cased Caddis
	12	Empty
	21	
April	4	Eggs (taken on redds)
	6	Eggs (taken in runs)
	5	Early Black Stonefly Nymphs (3 full)
	18	No Significant Amounts of Food
	33	
Study Total =	96 Fish	

Pobst's Feeding Research

From their sample, Pobst found that the fall fish fed on two things—salmon eggs and Caddis larvae. Some fish gorged while others only took a dozen or so pieces of food. Ray Schmidt, a steelhead guide, reported seeing fish so full of green caddis larvae that larvae were dribbling out of their mouths. Winter caught steelhead had tiny black stonefly nymphs in their stomachs. Spring caught steelhead again fed on eggs—their own, and eggs of suckers. They also fed on large brown and black stonefly nymphs, and caddis larvae dislodged from the stones by the activities of spawning fish. The guides also found steelhead with *Hexagenia* nymphs, but only one steelhead was found to have taken a minnow. *Note the sidebar.*

The evidence is clear that over half the fish caught had only traces or no food in them. But please realize that these numbers represent only the fish that were *caught*. Feeding fish are much more likely to be caught than the non-feeding fish. This means that the percentages of feeding fish in this sample must be larger than the number of feeding fish in the river at any one time. Realize also that happy fish are the most likely of all the fish to strike. They will likely have food in their stomachs too because they are sampling almost every new thing that comes down with the current.

Stale Fish

The ambition of Great Lakes fly fisherman is to catch not only the happy and feeding fish, but also the "stale" fish. Most of the time a migrant salmon or steelhead spends in the river it has a stale attitude. If fish are stale ninety percent of the time they are in the river, then we would have to ignore them ninety percent of the time. Not a favorable idea. Great Lakes flies and techniques were developed with the specific intent of catching these reluctant migrants.

Stale fish are the most unwilling fish to strike a fly, lure or bait. "Stale" defines their mental condition. A migratory fish in perfect physical condition can be stale because of many reasons. Steelhead and salmon become stale when they are completely intent on spawning. Others become stale because of heavy fishing pressure or painful encounters with anglers. Stale fish can include fish that have been caught and released. Others become stale because of unfavorable water temperatures, such as water that is too cold in winter and spring, or too hot in summer for Skamania steelhead.

> *Great Lakes fly fishermen experiment with different flies and techniques to increase success. They are less inhibited about breaking tradition, which has produced many fly fishing innovations*

Stale fish are the opposite of happy fish. Happy fish are content and stress-free while stale fish are stressed and discontent. Happy fish recreate by experimenting and trying new things. Stale fish are reluctant to try even the known events such as eating a nymph. It is much the same reason that there are very few golf courses in Ethiopia. You have to be comfortable in every other area before you go looking for entertainment or recreation. If a fish feels insecure about its life, or if the water temperature puts stress on it, then it is much less willing to chase something across the river or hit a fly.

Jim Johnson said, "If the fish is barely on the edge of survival, it is looking for the basics. In the fish's case that is a break for the current, good water temperatures, and enough food to stay alive. In the middle of spawning, the food aspect is a non-factor. Then the males are just looking for a female to spawn with and some good shelter from the current."

When the fish get stale the Northwestern fly fishermen stop catching them with their usual techniques. It is rare to constantly find pods of fresh, porpoising happy fish. But when you do, they'll hit anything, you don't need any type of refined technique to catch them. You can throw a chartreuse egg out there and you have them. That reaction is common for steelhead in October but not in the spring, unless you get into a pod of fresh fish that are just a couple days out of the big lake. Stale fish—on the contrary—are *contrary,* and if you cast that same chartreuse egg into a run you can spook a whole pod of stale steelhead.

In the spring, the steelhead darken and change much faster than in autumn. Fall fish stay happy for a few weeks before they turn stale. In the spring, however, steelhead get into the spawning mood quickly and lose interest in anything else. Once they go into spawning mode, the only option left is to provoke a strike with a defensive territorial reflex. As we will see in Chapter Three, the best way to create that territorial reaction is much different from the Northwestern method of casting a giant minnow imitation or a big Woolly Bugger.

Four Reasons Salmon and Steelhead Strike Flies

There are four basic reasons why migratory fish strike flies: Aggression/Irritation, Reflex/Protection, Feeding, and Playful/Experimentation. Fish with different attitudes strike flies for different reasons.

Aggression/Irritation: The aggression/irritation strikes come from fish that are on redds and become irritated at an intrusion. Or they are simply aggressive toward anything in the area—such as a huge male dominating a redd. This strike can be confused with those of fresh fish that take flies for experimentation. Irritation is the *least* reliable of the reasons to rely upon for catching steelhead.

Reflex/Protection: The reflex-protection strike comes from a fish that sees a nymph drifting down the river and basically ignores it until the nymph suddenly darts in front of its face. Then the fish can either dodge it or swallow it.

Steelhead take real nymphs in the river by reflex, like you swat a mosquito. You feel a mosquito on your arm, you often swat it without any interruption in your conversation. It's a stimulus/response activity—you feel a mosquito (stimulus), you swat (response). When steelhead return to their natal rivers, they see the nymphs they ate during their juvenile period. Confronted continually by drifting nymphs, they build a reflex response to take them. When a natural-looking nymph contains a hook, it surprises them—like someone who feels a mosquito, swats at it, and is stung by a bee. A steelhead's response to the sting of a hook—shock, panic, leaping hysteria—is not unlike the actions of someone stung by a bee.

The strength of this reflex response was proved one afternoon when Jim Johnson and I fished together at the Beaver Dam on the Pere Marquette River. I hooked a bright, eight-pound hen steelhead on a Hare's Ear Nymph; the fight took us downriver before she was netted. When I released her, she swam into a clear, nine foot deep pool. Fishing that pool, Jim drifted a Hare's Ear Nymph in front of her, and she took it. This was only a few minutes after I had hooked her on an identical fly. Jim landed the tired fish easily and released her again. Her strong reflex response initiated her taking the second fly.

> *Migratory fish strike flies for four reasons: Aggression/Irritation, Reflex/Protection, Feeding, and Playful/Experimentation*

The protection aspect of the reflex/protection strike comes from fish that are protecting their territory. It is much like having someone surprise you by throwing an ink pen across the table at you. You had not suspected that the pen was any threat but your instantaneous reflex response is to protect your face. Steelhead and salmon respond the same way. Except the fish do not have hands to swat it away. They only have their mouths, so their protective reflex is to grab it. That happens quickly before the fish realizes it. That is their instinctive, reflex reaction. After they realize their mistake they try to spit out the fly as quickly as possible. That is your chance to set the hook.

"You won't have much time to react to a strike in that situation," Jim Johnson said. "You can really tell the difference in a run if the fish are feeding, you're getting takes and thump, pull, pull, pull. They are chewing the fly and taking it right down. With these instantaneous takes, the fish spit out the fly as quickly as possible. Then you think, *Oh, that was my shot and I missed him.*

> **Fish with different attitudes strike flies for different reasons**

Feeding: The third reason salmon and steelhead strike flies is to feed. As we discussed earlier, feeding fish are most likely just in from a big lake, happy fish, summer-run fish or fall-run fish. Winter fish also feed some but less so because of the stress of the frigid water. The spring run of steelhead gets very little time to feed because they go quickly into spawning behavior. But females on redds seem prone to taking nymphs even while actively spawning.

Western guides, like Dave Hall of the North Umpqua, have learned to use "buggy patterns" when the traditional methods fail. Hall suggests three aquatic insects: the Golden Stone, the October Caddis, and the A.P. Flash Black Nymph. In *Advanced Fly Fishing for Steelhead*, Hall claims, "These flies represent insects that are prevalent in the North Umpqua river system that steelhead are familiar with because they were part of their diet when they were juvenile fish. But I'm not trying to match the hatch in any kind of traditional sense. I started fishing *natural buggy* patterns when the standard traditional patterns were not producing."

Playful/Experimentation: Happy fish have a playful, relaxed, comfortable attitude that allows them energy and attention to squander. However, happy fish also strike for the other three reasons. They willingly feed on nymphs drifting with the current. They maul large, bright streamers that provoke them. They gladly smack any fly that bounces into their noses by reflex or protection.

Happy fish are like the reflex chasing of a Harris' Hawk. A hawk's brain thinks, *If any quarry flees quickly, then I can catch it.* "Sarah," my 2-pound Harris Hawk, often chased and grabbed a full-grown whitetail deer, *if* it flushed from the prairie grass and bolted off like a frightened cottontail rabbit.

Some fish hit flies simply because they are in the same river—just for fun. But feeding fish will not move far to take flies in this manner. Feeding steelhead and salmon often take flies almost as selectively as brown trout. Sometimes you have to be as discriminating as a brown trout fisherman to catch feeding steelhead. A fish with a stale attitude would never dream of striking a fly that the happy fish mauls instantly. A stale fish may also refuse a perfect imitation of a natural nymph, delivered to it with a drag-free drift. The stale fish will also avoid anything it suspects as an irritation or provocation. That leaves only the reflex/protection strike for these reluctant fish. More on that in every chapter.

The Stages of Great Lakes Flies

As Bob Nicholson's story showed, Great Lakes fly fishermen began by casting streamers in different colors and sizes to salmon and steelhead. Then they went to Spring Wigglers—a nymph of sorts—in different colors and then to yarn egg patterns—Glo Bugs. Stage one in the Great Lakes fly evolution was streamers and spawn imitations in different colors and sizes.

In stage two, fly anglers tied and tried very realistic nymphs to catch the feeding fish. But only thirty percent of the *caught* fish had any food in them at all. The percentage of fish—of the whole population in the river—that were eating must have been much smaller because the feeding fish are more likely to take a fly. As we saw earlier, a feeding fish is more likely to be caught. Therefore feeding fish will make up a greater percentage of the *caught sample* of any creel survey. The percentage of feeding fish in the study results must be higher than their real percentage. If you are targeting feeding fish only, you are fishing for at most thirty percent of the fish in the river. This thirty percent is fish that take food sporadically, the percentage of fish that actively feed or gorge themselves is much lower. Therefore, to pursue only the actively feeding fish you limit your fishing to maybe only fifteen percent of the fish in the river.

In the third stage the anglers sought to catch the seventy percent-plus of the fish in the river that are not eating anything. The goal is to select a fly that can attract a strike from all three types of fish that are in the river. Flies like the Sparrow Nymph appear enough like a natural food item to trigger a response from feeding fish. It is active enough with soft hackle and philo-plume to trigger an aggressive-reflex from a stale fish, and a happy fish is just pleased to see it in the same river and will smack it for *that* reason. A P.M. Wiggler fly tied with marabou and Caddis Larva fly tied with soft hackle also solicit these same responses. These flies get closer to the one hundred percent mark and your fishing suc-

cess increases. Instead of fishing for only the fifteen percent actively feeding, or the thirty percent taking small amounts of food, now anglers try to get closer to that one hundred percent by adding the philoplume, the soft hackle and the marabou tails.

Tom Johnson, Jim's brother, who is also a fly fishing guide and co-owner of the Pere Marquette Lodge, developed one of the first patterns specifically created with this philosophy in mind. He called it the P.M. Wiggler. It is a Hex-nymph pattern using marabou for the back and tail, it seems like a cross between a nymph and a Woolly Bugger. Tom took out the long thorax hackle and put in an ostrich herl to give it tight motion close to the body. This imitates the tight movement of a *Hexagenia's* gills. When the P.M. Wiggler is dead-drifting it has a nymph action.

"The ideal fly in my opinion," Tom Johnson said. "Here is a fly that looks very much like a food item while it is dead-drifting. Then when the weight touches the bottom it can turn into an aggressive looking fly with undulations. Any kind of current movement will trigger a reaction from the fly. Soft hackle, philoplume and marabou are two of the best things for that. Marabou is the very best. While

Reflex-Response Strike

**Lance Wiertalla (left) and his son, Brent, with a pair of
Pink Salmon caught on "Reflex Strikes"**

fishing, I will always have on at least one fly with either marabou or philoplume in it. That gives the fly lots of action even with just a slight eddy or side current. That can give you what you wouldn't get otherwise."

> *Sometimes you have to be as
> discriminating as a brown trout
> fisherman to catch feeding steelhead*

Over the years, at least three times another fisherman and I have caught the *same* steelhead within a few minutes on identical flies. Jim Johnson and I caught the same hen steelhead as I mentioned earlier. That hen was caught on a number six Hare's Ear Nymph. The fly may not have looked identical to the fish, because the second hook came up when she was in a pool with less light than the redd. That incident certainly shows that a fish took the fly

when she did not want to take it. She had no desire to eat that fly, and she knew that particular fly was not good to eat.

On the other two occasions the fly must have looked identical to the fish. The second time was a hen that twice took an olive Caddis Larva off the same redd. The third time was a male steelhead, caught on a Hex-nymph, once off a redd and secondly by Chuck Emmeret from the shallow run behind the redd.

Like the first two occasions that fish did not *want* to take a fly. But it did anyway.

Why?

The first key was having the right fly.

Secondly was provoking them with the right fly fishing technique . . .

But that is Chapter Three.

Drift-Fly-Fishing

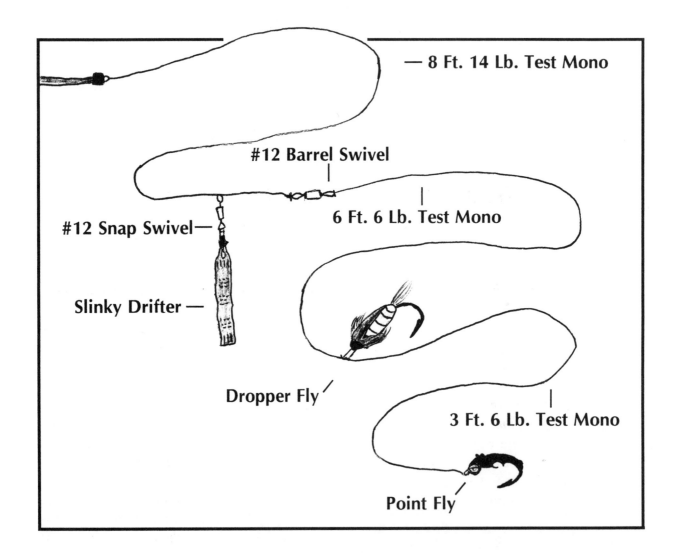

— 8 Ft. 14 Lb. Test Mono

#12 Barrel Swivel

#12 Snap Swivel —

6 Ft. 6 Lb. Test Mono

Slinky Drifter —

Dropper Fly

3 Ft. 6 Lb. Test Mono

Point Fly

"Flies In Their Face"

Great Lakes Fly Fishing Techniques

You can cast the right flies all day and never hook a fish. Often ninety percent of the fish in the river won't move even a few inches to take a fly, much less move a couple feet. Most fish will *never* swim across the river to strike a fly.

For ninety percent of steelhead and salmon, you must *go after them*. They will not come to you. The difference between success and complete failure can be as little as nine inches. Considering the depth and width of the Great Lake tributaries, that is not very reassuring. But it is true.

Most of the time you have to target your flies into a smaller strike zone than a pitcher in a midget baseball league. Failure means the fish will not even notice your fly, much less strike it.

Unfortunately, that is not all. The flies must also be presented into that tiny strike zone *at the right speed*. Something more akin to a

knuckleball than a fast ball. The flies must mimic the speed of the current where the fish are holding. No easy feat since the top current—through which your line must pass—is much faster and tends to pull your flies quickly downriver and to one side. That is a "slider" pitch to the strike zone, or in more technical fly fishing terms, the fly has "drag." The fly is moving side-to-side in the strike zone. Most steelhead and salmon will refuse such an awkward "pitch."

Oddly enough, the right fly with the wrong technique may be a greater disability than casting the wrong fly with the right technique. At least in the latter case, the fish has to refuse the fly. All fly fishing techniques are not created equal. When you use the wrong technique, the fish will never notice the fly. To get the flies into the strike zone a fly fisherman can select from three basic techniques: Traditional fly fishing techniques; Heavyweight shootingheads; and Drift-fly-fishing technique—using a Slinky Drifter. Each has its own strengths and weaknesses.

Traditional Fly Fishing Techniques employ a sinktip, full-sinking or floating fly line where the weight of the line loads the rod. The fastest sink-rate currently available with these lines is only 12 inches per second. Some consider floating lines with a strike indicator and with split-shot crimped to the leader as traditional fly fishing. Others consider using a small foam bobber as a strike indicator as traditional fly fishing as well. Of course, using a Spey rod with Spey flies is a traditional fly fishing technique.

These methods are the most enjoyable ways to fish but are often the least effective in the conditions on Great Lakes tributaries, because they are the least effective for catching stale fish. Traditional methods can be just as effective if you are fishing a pod of happy fish, which is what these methods target.

Short, Heavy Shootingheads are condensed sinking shootingheads whose sink-rate is faster than any traditional method. For example, the 30-inch long Osprey™ shootinghead has a 28-inches-per-second sink-rate and has been the most effective of this type of technique. The Os210 Osprey™ shootinghead has the weight of 30-foot of a 7-weight fly line in 30-inches.

These short, heavy shootingheads allow for some of the joy of traditional casting and great roll casting. They are also more effective than the traditional methods, because they get the flies down quicker. This method is midway between the traditional and Drift-fly-fishing. It casts more like the traditional methods but its effectiveness leans more toward the Drift-fly-fishing technique.

Drift-fly-fishing—the most non-traditional of all the Great Lakes fly fishing methods—employs a fly rod and fly reel but uses a shooting fly line, flat monofilament, a barrel swivel and Slinky Drifters (or split-shot) to load the rod and pull the flies down. Because of its effectiveness it is also the most popular Great Lakes technique. However, it is frequently charged with "not being fly fishing at all." This prejudice is not unlike that in the Rockies against the worm fishing on the San Juan River. Fishermen use the San Juan worm fly on a rigging with split-shot that is dead-drifted almost at the angler's feet. Over the years we have heard less and less objection as that method proved its incredible effectiveness, though some still grumble. In that way Drift-fly-fishing is no different.

The main mistake that anglers make with these three types of techniques is that they think that they are completely interchangeable. That on any given day, any method will be effective. This is not the case.

Strike Indicator Fishing

Techniques Are Not Interchangeable

The attitude of targeted fish and the river conditions will determine what technique will be the most effective on that day. In the Great Lakes much confusion exists because fly fishermen are experimenting with many different techniques. The basic misconception is that all these techniques are interchangeable. They wrongly think, *Today I could use any of these*

Hump-backed Salmon

techniques—whatever I am in the mood for—and be successful. Deep-nymphing with Drift-fly-fishing is effective all the time no matter what the conditions. But it is not necessarily the *most* effective in every condition. There are a few conditions when it would be better to go another way—but those are very few. For instance, summer exploring for fish with the Teeny 400 sinktip line or an Osprey™ shootinghead with streamers allows you to cover lots of water quickly to find a pod of active fish. The summer fish are generally happy fish that will hit swinging streamers.

In certain conditions the other methods—such as Osprey™ shootinghead, Spey rods,

sinktips, or strike indicators—have a good chance of being successful. However, often there are days when they have very little chance of success. Then Drift-fly-fishing becomes your only option if you want to catch fish consistently.

Understanding the different techniques and when they are most effective will help you decide which method has the greatest chance of being successful that day. When you encounter a pod of fresh fish in a pool you can say, "This is a good time to fish a big Spey rod and a big Spey attractor fly—swinging flies through the pool." But on redds in late April while fishing to harassed, spooked fish, Spey flies will fail.

"You may want to try some weird method for a couple hours *just to learn it*," Jim Johnson said. "We do that when we fish on our own. As a guide, I never fish any area unless I'm one hundred percent convinced that it holds fish. Maximizing hookups means using lighter leader than most people, and by using the fly fishing technique that will hook the most fish *that* day. The most effective technique that works well—if not the best—in every situation is Drift-fly-fishing with Slinky Drifters."

Drift-fly-fishing

The popularity of Drift-fly-fishing is determined by its effectiveness in getting all three types of fish to strike, whether they are happy, feeding or stale. This technique is especially successful on stale fish.

As we have seen, migrating salmon and steelhead are stale most of the time they are in the river, especially as they get closer to spawning. Therefore, to consistently catch fish, you must solicit strikes from stale fish. Stale fish will not move to take a fly, therefore you must confront them with a fly using a "passive-aggressive" method.

That is where the Drift-fly-fishing technique gets so effective. The closer you get to spawning time, the more effective it gets because the flies go right into those spots after the fish, instead of making them come out after the flies.

> *Drift-fly-fishing—the most non-traditional fly fishing method—employs a fly rod and fly reel but uses a shooting fly line, flat monofilament, a barrel swivel and Slinky Drifters to pull the flies down*

Happy fish give you the most freedom with flies and techniques. Feeding fish are more restrictive by demanding natural patterns and a dead-drift resulting from your technique. Stale fish are the most demanding. They won't move to strike a fly, they won't take a fly for food, and they flee if they see anything unnatural coming their way. The stale fish are the ones that dictated the Great Lakes evolution in steelhead flies and techniques. Drift-fly-fishing is a direct result of their persnickety attitude.

Jim Johnson explains, "The easier it is for the fish to eat the fly than to *not* eat it, the less active the fish has to be to strike. The drift-fishing technique will catch every fish in the river that isn't spooked so badly that it turns and runs any time it gets any kind of confrontation."

Passive-Aggressive Fly Fishing

The best way to create an instinctive, territorial strike is to use "passive-aggressive" fly fishing. To explain the passive-aggressive method, Jim Johnson shared a grizzly bear analogy.

> *Keep the tippet long enough to not spook the fish and as short as possible for the river conditions*

"Grizzly bears are not afraid of anything in their own environment," Jim Johnson explained. "But when a very intrusive person—that's definitely out of place—comes through its area, the bear generally *avoids a confrontation*. It's the same for steelhead. Occasionally, you will find an extremely aggressive male steelhead that's chasing everything. Then I put on a big egg sucking leech and they swim over and smack it. That exception just proves the rule. The fish that does that is one in a hundred—if that many. It's like grizzly bears, maybe one out of a hundred will come over and maul you when they see you from a distance.

"Think of it like this," Jim continued. "You're walking down an Alaskan river and you spot the bear. The grizzly is feeding on the bank, minding his own business. If you crawl across the tundra on your hands and knees, sneak up within five feet of the bear, then jump up and shout 'Boo!' he'll maul you every time. That's not the way to avoid getting being eaten by a grizzly. If you see a bear (that has enough food, is minding his own business, and doesn't particularly want to eat you), and want to avoid getting mauled, hang a cowbell around your neck and walk loudly through that territory. The bear can hear you coming and see you from a distance, and usually this content bear will avoid the confrontation whenever possible.

"That's what steelhead do, *they avoid confrontation whenever possible*. The occasional

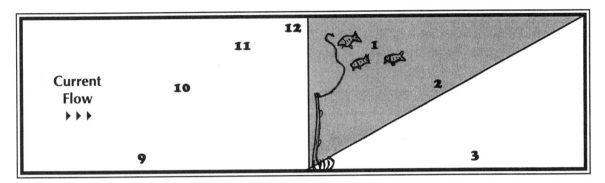

Strike Zone for Left to Right Current

Strike Zone is the shaded area between 12 and 2

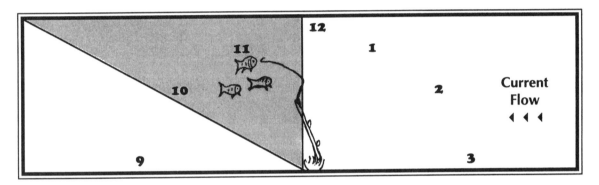

Strike Zone for Right to Left Current

Strike Zone is the shaded area between 10 and 12

grizzly bear will still charge over and maul you. And the occasional steelhead will swim over and maul a fly as well. But it is equally as occasional. If you cast a huge chartreuse streamer and run it through a redd, the majority of steelhead will choose to avoid that confrontation if they see it coming.

"My goal is to sneak that fly down through the tundra until it gets within that range where the steelhead is going to protect its territory no matter what, and then have it jump up and yell, 'Boo!'"

That's passive-aggressive fly fishing.

It uses small natural flies that won't alert the fish—especially stale fish—to its presence until it's too late. The fly comes down through the fish's strike zone and the fish thinks, *This is no big deal, I've seen hundreds of these stone-fly nymphs go past.* Then, as the nymph comes close to the steelhead, the Slinky Drifter—which is way over to the side out of the fish's vision—touches the bottom. When the Slinky strikes the bottom this fly jumps up and "attacks" the fish. The "attack" is that the fly does something unnatural and uncharacteristic for what the steelhead had expected. It jumped up and screamed, "Boo!"

The instantaneous reaction of that fish—if everything is set up just right—is to grab the fly. You cannot deliberately create that situation, so you make several casts until it happens accidentally.

The only obstacle preventing you from catching that fish is that you spook the fish with a cast. The fish will spook because you get the Slinky too close, or you splash too loudly, or your cast lands too close to the fish, or the fish sees the rod waving around, or your flies are wearing "cowbells." If the fly looks unnatural to the fish it will spook. Once a fish sees a cowbell and is alerted to your presence, it becomes much less likely to strike, even if it does not leave the run or redd. The fly must look so natural that it does not alert the fish. If you cast the flies and the fish moves out of the way as the flies come down, your rig is wearing a cowbell. It is just like that bear moving out of the way to avoid confrontation.

The cowbell could be too heavy of a leader, too big a fly, or too unnatural of a pattern. If you have a perfect imitation and it is unattached to leader and weight, the fly will not behave strangely. The goal is to make it appear completely natural and get as close to the fish as possible, until that last instance when it is too late. This is especially true for the inactive, non-feeding, nonplayful—stale—fish.

Swinging streamers through a run with a West Coast technique is a cowbell to stale fish. The traditional West Coast techniques are rarely used to pursue feeding or inactive fish. Those techniques pursue only playful, happy fish. When the fish have been in the river a few weeks the West Coast techniques stop working and stop catching fish.

Especially for Stale Fish

The rigging for Drift-fly-fishing begins with a shooting fly line, then tie on a butt section of flat 12 or 15-pound monofilament at least nine-feet long. Then slide the butt section through the top swivel of a black snap swivel, so the snap hangs down. Next tie a barrel swivel to the end of the butt section. The snap swivel will slide freely between the fly line and the barrel swivel. To the other end of the barrel swivel tie on your tippet material of 4, 5, 6, or 8-pound-test monofilament, about six feet long, then attach your first fly.

Tie more tippet material into the eye of your dropper fly, then tie on the point fly two to four

feet away. Finally, open the snap and poke it through the cord of the appropriately weighted Slinky Drifter. Then begin casting.

> *If the water is deeper than 2 or 3 feet or the current is faster than 6 or 7 miles/hour, switch to Drift-fly-fishing to tremendously improve the success*

Dead-drifting your flies through redds, runs and pools produces the most strikes. To cast to spawning steelhead, for example, stand facing across the current so that the fish are between 12 o'clock and "two hours" downriver. If the river flows from your left to the right, then 12 o'clock is directly across the current toward the opposite bank. Wade in the current until the fish are below 12 o'clock but above 2 o'clock (if the current flows from right to left, put the fish between 12 and 10 o'clock). This area becomes your dead-drift zone and consequently your strike zone.

Attach a Slinky Drifter to your snap swivel, then cast so the Slinky Drifter hits the water 12 to 15 feet upriver of the steelhead. Hold your rod tip high and keep the line tight to the Drifter. You will feel the Drifter tapping the bottom as your rig nears the steelhead. If you do not feel it tapping the bottom, put on a heavier Slinky. If the Slinky drags to a stop or slows to a very slow bounce, put on a lighter Slinky. Also make sure the Drifter begins hitting the bottom six feet upstream of the steelhead so the flies get down to the fish's eye level.

> *The only obstacle preventing you from catching that fish is that you spook it with a cast*

If the line *pauses* any time while the flies drifts through the strike zone—set the hook. You either caught a rock or had a steelhead strike. If you try guessing which pause is a rock and which is a fish, you'll miss some strikes—I have.

If it pauses, set the hook.

Casting this rig is not traditional flycasting. First, pull in the fly line until it is within six inches of the end of the shooting line, then lift the Slinky Drifter out of the water. Position the rod 180° from where you want the cast. Cast forward, stop the rod high and release the fly line when the Drifter pulls at the line. Though it takes a little practice, you'll soon cast into—and from—very tight places where traditional flycasting is impossible.

Another effective method omits the snap swivel and leaves a three inch tag-end of the knot at the top of the barrel swivel. Instead of Slinky Drifters, crimp Number 5 or 7 split-shot to the tag-end. Add split-shot until it pulls your flies into the strike zone near the bottom of the river. I used this method for years until I began making Slinky Drifters. The Drifters are not lost as often to the logs and rocks, and provide a sensitive *ticking* along the river bottom, which makes it easier to detect a strike. Also, Slinkys spook less fish because they produce less noise and flash.

Traditional Techniques

The traditional techniques can be very effective, especially with happy fish and in shallow water conditions or while searching for pods of summer or fall run steelhead. These are the techniques that get abundant press and are therefore well known.

Sinktip lines and full-sinking lines work for the same situations but every fly fishing guide I spoke with said the submerged fly line spooks some fish.

Here a long leader is preferable and a lead-eye fly—like a lead-eye Woolly Bugger—may help get the flies down into the strike zone. The Teeny lines and Spey gear work best for the situations and fish they were created for—fresh

Lars Rishaug with summer run steelhead

fish, happy fish, summer-run and fall-run fish.

Some Western anglers find success with traditional techniques and nymphs. Fishing writer Brad Jackson of Redding, California, wrote, "My baptism in the merits of dead-drifting nymphs occurred eleven years ago on California's Trinity River. Previously I had little success with Trinity steelhead when the water temperatures plummeted in late fall. Steelhead are less aggressive in really cold water, and standard attractor wets, even fish on sinking lines, provide inconsistent action. After a futile morning using traditional searching methods with attractor wets, I switched to the heaviest fly in my box—a stonefly nymph triple-wrapped with lead. On the first, deep, natural drift the line drew tight. I raised the rod, and an 8-pound fish thrashed to the surface, shaking its head. I landed that fat hen and two more sleek fish of about four pounds each before that day ended."

Floating Line and Long Leaders

Floating line with a very long leader can be quite effective for redds when you put a couple split-shot in front of the flies. If the water gets deeper than two or three feet or the current gets faster than six or seven miles an hour, switch to the Drift-fly-fishing and it improves the success tremendously.

In two feet of water and slower current, a long leader and a couple of BB shots will be very effective. Keep the fly line out of the fish's field of view by using a leader at least 12 feet long.

Once you begin fishing in three or four feet of water the floating line method makes it difficult to control your drifts. The floating line works best if you can see the fish and watch them react to the fly. With this method, your sensitivity to the strike has diminished greatly when compared to Drift-fly-fishing. You cannot feel strikes as well, so watching for strikes becomes critical. The weight of the fly line also deadens your feel, because the fish must also move the additional weight of the fly line before you can sense its strike. With this method there will be sag in the line, which further decreases your chances of feeling a strike.

> *The traditional West Coast techniques are rarely used to pursue feeding or inactive fish*

If you use a 7 or 8-weight fly line you may never feel a strike. By the time you feel it, the fish is already hooked and on. He has either spit out the fly or hooked himself, because the droop in the line will be feet, not inches—as it is in the Drift-fly-fishing method. The experience will be more visual, using a strike indicator or a length of chartreuse Amnesia line tied into your rig. It is most effective to fish shallow enough locations where you can see the fish and how they respond to the flies.

The Best Time To Use Traditional Fly Fishing

The strike indicator technique will not bring the fly downstream in a completely natural motion. The strike indicator moves at the speed of the surface film, which is faster than the bottom current. The fly moves through the strike zone quicker than the natural food items. The fly flows past the fish in a straight line. If the nymph just passes by naturally and goes on its way, the only fish that will take it is either the curious fish or the feeding fish.

In the third week of October, the steelhead come in fresh from the big lake so there are very few steelhead—if any—that are inactive or nonfeeding fish. You can then target one type of fish and be the most successful. Fish a chartreuse egg and cover lots of water, and using a big streamer will get strikes from pods of aggressive or feeding fish. On these fall days you have the best of both worlds; the traditional methods work well—you can cover water quickly and the fish you encounter are happy fish.

If the pods of fish are feeding, the strike indicator is a deadly technique, because the fish will move up and take a fly. You do not have to hit the fish in the face. Strike indicator fishing keeps the nymphs up off the bottom so the fish see the fly from further away. You can cover many different kinds of pools that way, including those with rubble on the bottom. However, if the fish are not actively feeding and aggressively going after food, you won't catch as many fish.

Short, Heavy Shootingheads

The evolution to the short, heavy fast-sinking shootinghead began with a quest to get away from Drift-fly-fishing and toward traditional fly casting without losing the effectiveness. The Osprey™ shootinghead and other homemade shootingheads lean in that direction. By their nature they are heavy—the weight of a 30-foot section of fly line in 30-inches of

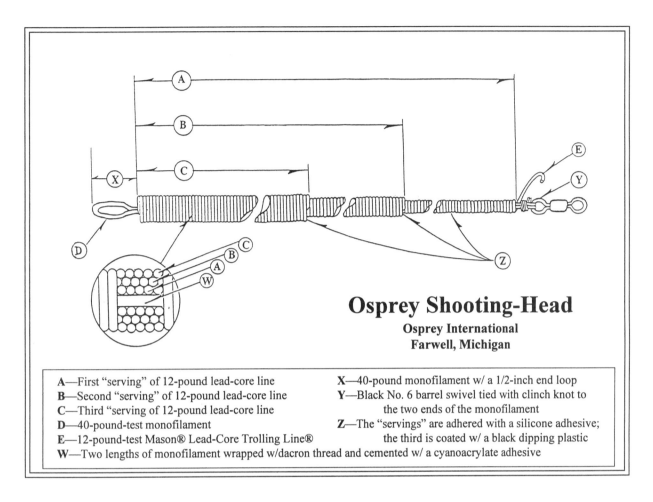

Osprey Shooting-Head
Osprey International
Farwell, Michigan

A—First "serving" of 12-pound lead-core line
B—Second "serving" of 12-pound lead-core line
C—Third "serving of 12-pound lead-core line
D—40-pound-test monofilament
E—12-pound-test Mason® Lead-Core Trolling Line®
W—Two lengths of monofilament wrapped w/dacron thread and cemented w/ a cyanoacrylate adhesive

X—40-pound monofilament w/ a 1/2-inch end loop
Y—Black No. 6 barrel swivel tied with clinch knot to
       the two ends of the monofilament
Z—The "servings" are adhered with a silicone adhesive;
       the third is coated w/ a black dipping plastic

shootinghead. That is 12 times heavier per inch! And they sink accordingly. Traditional sinktip lines are proud to get up to 12 inches-per-second. The Osprey™ sinks at 28-inches-per-second for the Os210 Model for flyrods 6 through 9-weight.

The shootingheads can be cast with traditional fly-casting techniques or with a modified roll-cast. These shootingheads pull the flies down into deep pools and down quickly in fast water at spawning redds. They provide the "feel" of drifting flies on a sinking fly line instead of the "tapping" of a Slinky Drifter on the river bottom. Fishing with a condensed sinking shootinghead keeps the angler tight to the flies, allows fishing for suspended fish in pools, and protects the line from snags.

Many Great Lakes fly fishermen have been and will continue to experiment with creating sinking shootingheads. So far, little has been

written about those experiments. Here is a short history of one shootinghead's development. This may guide and assist others in the pursuit of the perfect shootinghead.

One April, Dr. Jim Watt, Tom Jared and I went steelhead fly fishing together. Doc and I used Drift-fly-fishing gear and Tom used drift gear with monofilament on his fly reel.

"I hate split-shot," Tom Jared said, "Isn't there another way we can do this?"

"Well, I've used a lead-core leader made by Orvis," I replied, "But they're too light for this application. Maybe there's something else we can do to create our own sinking shootingheads? Let's work on it."

I was thinking about using Cortland LC-13™ vinyl coated lead-core line to create a quick sinking shootinghead. Still, I didn't made a prototype shootinghead until September, when we planned a trip to Ontario for the Pink salmon run. I made one shootinghead of 15-feet of Cortland lead-core with two braided end-loops and tested it on Dr. Watt's pond. It failed. It was too long to manage. When I shortened it to 7-foot, it was more manageable and I hooked a large bass. The 7-foot length was the weight of the average Slinky Drifter, but the uniform sink created a sag in the line. A problem.

At this time Tom Jared asked why Mason Lead Core® metered trolling line (for bait casting reels) wouldn't work for this application, though it doesn't have the weight-volume-per-foot needed.

While in Ontario Tom McNerney suggested that we create the end-loops with the Cortland lead-core by using shrink wrap to loop each end. Then we realized a partial solution to the sag problem—"double back the lead-core 18-inches and shrink wrap that 18-inches." This created a *heavy tip* shootinghead and shortened it to six feet long.

> *Fishing with a condensed sinking shootinghead keeps the angler tight to the flies, allows fishing for suspended fish in pools, and protects the line from snags*

When the Farwell crew arrived the next day, we had made these heavy-tipped shootingheads for everyone. For the next week, I experimented with different combinations of heavy tips—like tripling the Cortland lead-core for 18-inches, then putting five lengths at least 6-inches. These heavy-tipped shootingheads were effective fishing tools that could be cast with traditional fly fishing techniques, but they were very stiff because of the multiple strands of lead-core bound by shrink wrap.

One day, after our return home to Farwell, I watched while Tom Jared was serving a bow-string ("serving" is wrapping a line tightly around a bowstring) at his sports shop—The Farwell Trading Post. As I watched him, we

discussed the shootingheads and their merits and deficiences. The stiffness was the major concern. We didn't resolve anything then, but a couple of hours later I stopped back at Tom's and said, "Picture this. Take Cortland lead-core with end-loops and stretch it like a bowstring. Put 12-pound-test Mason Lead Core® trolling line on your bowstring server and wrap the shootinghead with the lead line. It will be heavy, yet very flexible."

Tom smiled.

> *Keep the weight away from the fish to remove any connection between the weight and the flies*

He created a "power server" out of his fishing line winder and used a 30-inch length of 40-pound monofilament as a core. Tom then served (wrapped) the 12-pound-test Mason Lead Core® line around the monofilament. He created the first tapered condensed sinking shootingheads in a great variety of weights. We fished with all of them and settled on three sizes that fit all river conditions—110-gr, 160-gr, 210-gr.

At first, we had an end-loop of both ends of the shootinghead but the Osprey™ tumbles as it progresses downriver. That put a spin in the fly line, so a barrel swivel at the fly line end corrected this. One dynamic of the shootinghead is that its length and diameter allow the current to push it along the bottom *at the speed of the current*. This keeps the flies moving at the correct speed. Because of this hydrodynamic these shootingheads work well for several situations without changing sizes. You can fish the whole day without changing your shootinghead. You can fish pools, runs and redds with equal effectiveness, especially if the deepest water is no deeper than five to eight feet. Deeper than that these shootingheads become proportionally less effective.

Originally, we attached the tippet to the shootinghead with a loop-to-loop connection but we became convinced we were losing too much line strength with that knot. Now we put a swivel at *both* ends of the shootinghead so we can tie the tippet directly to the swivel.

The Osprey™ shootingheads are a compromise between the Slinky method and traditional technique. Ospreys™ allow for more of the *feel* of flycasting and fishing, but they are more effective at hooking salmon and steelhead.

We found they work well in areas where you do not need a long drag-free drift, such as on redds and shallow runs. The Osprey™ is also effective for summer and fall fishing to cover lots of water by swinging streamers through runs. The Osprey™ is very effective on small enclosed rivers where a roll cast is necessary.

A long tippet is also required for the Osprey™ to keep it and the fly line out of the fish's panic zone. By "long tippet" we do not mean 18-inches, as is all too prevalent. If you get everything else right and screw up on the tippet— you're done.

Tippet Techniques

Someone, somewhere wrote that you can use an 18-inch tippet from your sinktip line or weight and that is all you need. Unfortunately, many have taken that as gospel. Because of the tippet length, too many fishermen have spent many fruitless days wondering why they were not catching fish. Yes, with an 18-inch tippet you will occasionally catch those aggressive fish that attack everything. But that is it. You will not effectively

catch feeding fish because the weight is too close to the nymph and the fly will not behave naturally. You will almost never catch the stale fish because the fish have learned that fly lines and weights mean trouble. Don't believe it? Just take off your flies and run your Slinky Drifter or split-shot *through* the fish. You will spook all the fish.

If you accidentally run the split-shot through the redd, that redd is useless for the next half hour. The farther you keep the weight from the flies, the better. "Split-shot is the worst because it's making noise as it goes down through the gravel," Jim Johnson said.

"Fish spook from the sound. My friend proved that to me by rubber coating some split-shot. We put rubber coated split-shot (painted

Tom Jared with a Chinook Salmon

in brown and olive camouflage) and regular split-shot on our leaders without flies. The third week of April, we went to the river when no one was there and we found fish all over the gravel. He bounced that split-shot through the

Two knots tied onto one fly

move away from flies ten feet before they reach them. If the fish see ten feet to the fly, they see ten feet to the Slinky as well.

The only tippet material I use is Maxima Ultra-Green and Chameleon. Ultra-Green is the only choice for most Great Lakes tributaries, its color takes away the glint of clear monofilament and it is very abrasion resistant. That is a huge plus for rocky rivers. I use Chameleon monofilament for rivers with a high level of tanic acid that colors the water.

fish. The rubber coated shot got much closer to the redds than plain split-shot. That is what convinced me to go completely to Slinky Drifters. I have never used split-shot since."

Slinky Drifters just slide through the gravel, rarely get caught up and are camouflaged. Some fish will even bite a Slinky. You increase your success by keeping the weight as far from the fish's information highway as possible. To a certain degree, the shorter the tippet the better control you have over the position of the flies. Also the quicker you will feel a strike and more likely get the hook set. Therefore, keep the tippet long enough to not spook the fish and as short as possible for the river conditions. That will vary from day to day. If the water is clear and the sun is really bright, that may be nine feet. Keep the weight at least four or five feet away from the flies, even when the water clarity is poor. Most of the time, fish with 7 or 8-feet between your weight and the flies. Try to keep the tippet as long as your rod from the weight to the last fly.

Keeping the weight away from the fish will remove the perception of any connection between the weight and the flies. The flies—it should appear to the fish—act completely disconnected from the weight. Fish can clearly see a great distance underwater, just watch fish

The Two Fly Technique

Unless special regulations disbar it, I always use two flies on my rig by tying a dropper fly as if it was the only fly. Then I tie tippet material again into that same eye. Two to three feet away I tie on the point fly. You can also tie on the first fly with a dropper line, but you will lose line strength. I have found no functional difference in the success rate of a fly tied "in-line" to the one tied as the point. I have caught the same number of fish on the dropper fly as on the point fly. Neither is a disadvantage. Generally, I tie the smaller fly on as the point fly, which allows it to move more naturally. I also tie a small point fly with a Rapala knot so that it can undulate more naturally in the current.

The double fly rig has several advantages, including:

- You get double the strikes by presenting twice as many flies to the fish.
- You are twice as likely to cast a fly that the fish will strike.
- Your "attraction zone" is twice as wide while drifting through the run or pool.
- You are twice as likely to have a fly drift correctly into the strike zone of the fish.

🕷 You can evaluate the effectiveness of different flies twice as quickly.

The second fly can also distract the fish's attention. When fishing two flies, one is a decoy. You determine the length of the tippet between the two flies by the distance the fish move from a fly that day. If the fish move over two feet from the fly, then put the second fly at two and a half feet. When the steelhead moves over and pauses, "Boo!" there is the second fly. The fish's first reflex is to grab the fly. Then it is too late to flee, so it strikes the fly. Fish don't have hands to swat it out of the way. As they grab the fly with their mouth, they quickly try to spit it out.

That is when the soft-bodied, soft-dubbed flies and the yarn get caught in their teeth and you get more time to set the hook. Yarn is the perfect material to build a fly. Egg flies stick like Velcro™ to steelhead and salmon teeth. This will not give you much extra time, maybe a quarter of a second. Putting Slinkies on a sliding swivel gives you another fraction of a second before the fish feels the resistance. This will often mean an extra fish or two a week. All these little things increase the percentages a small way, but they add up over a season.

Gear Selection

The best way to suggest gear is to list what to get "if I could only have one— God forbid—which would it be?" Please do not tell my wife that this list is even possible, much less that *I* created it.

If I could have only one rod to fish for every species of salmon and steelhead in Great Lakes tributaries, I would pick a 7 or 8-weight rod, 9.5 or 10 feet long with a "fast action." It must have a soft tip and a firm butt section. The soft tip protects the thin tippets and the firm butt section allows for fighting huge fish. For small salmon like Pinks, I prefer using a 4

Gear Selection

or 5-weight rod and a trout reel. This leads to some unintentional thrills as we will see later when we get to the Chinook salmon. For Kings, I prefer an 8 or even 9-weight rod. For Atlantics I use a 4 to 6-weight rod depending on where I am fishing for them. The two handed Spey rods are great fun on large rivers, especially for the St. Mary's Rapids in Ontario. For several years, I fished my father-in-law's 13-foot noodle rod converted into a flyrod and enjoyed its gentle casting and long reach. For a King salmon, ah . . . later.

If I could only have one reel, I would buy the best disk-drag reel I could afford. There are more disk-drag reels coming out each year and the quality and prices vary accordingly. The best reel for the money is the Scientific Angler System 2—the 6-7 weight model is my favorite. Of course, there is the Billy Pate . . .

> *The ideal fly looks very much like a food item while it is dead-drifting. Then when the weight touches the bottom it can turn into an aggressive looking fly with undulations. Any kind of current movement will trigger a reaction from the fly*

For Pink salmon I use a single action Orvis trout reel that I can palm. A disk-drag is necessary for any other salmon or steelhead if you are going to slow those brutes without breaking your tippet. Many fish have been lost because fishermen have held on to the reel handle or applied too much pressure while palming the reel. A quality disk-drag reel gives you the freedom to fight fish "on the reel." That leaves you free to focus on the fight, log jams, and wading downriver during the fight. Also I would buy two spare spools so that I could carry shooting line, shootingheads and traditional fly line. This puts all three of the fly fishing techniques at my fingertips all the time.

Polarized sunglasses are a *must* for fly fishing, especially if you are sight-fishing. I always carry at least two pairs. One dark pair works for very bright days, and the amber pair for overcast days, early morning, and late evening.

John Hunter taught me how to make a Slinky Drifter with camouflaged parachute cord (from Wal-Mart's camping section) and Number 4 Buck Shot (or ¼-inch steel bearings). Simply cut off a couple feet of parachute cord, pull out the core, then slip in lots of lead or

steel balls. Next light a candle, melt the end of the cord then clamp it off with pliers. Slide down the number of balls you want in that Slinky, cut off the cord, then melt and clamp that end. Repeat this process until you get a vast collection of Slinkies. I generally fill a 4 x 8-inch plastic box with Slinkies. I make some in sizes 2 through 8—the most frequently used sizes are 3 through 5.

A driftboat or a canoe is hardly a necessity, but I don't ever want to be without one again. They give access to the river that cannot be reached any other way. They also allow you to take along lots of plunder—a blessing and a curse—and sons, brothers, and friends. Rarely do we fish from the boat; we simply use it for access to the river and we wade to fish.

Depending on the season and the river, there are other requirements: chest-high neoprene waders (booted and felt soles), cleated sandals for waders, a knot tyer (more on that in Chapter 10), rain gear, gloves, hat, landing net, and a propane heater (for winter trips in the boat).

When I go downriver, I have all the rigging for Drift-fly-fishing, Osprey™ shooting-head and traditional fly fishing. Whatever the fish or the situation dictates as to the highest percentage method, I can be ready in minutes to fish.

That means hooking more fish no matter what season, as we will see in the next chapter.

Hot Summer Action
Fishing Summer Run Steelhead

Summer and steelhead seem to go together like Wile E. Coyote and Ernest Hemingway. The contradiction can be either a blessing or a curse.

In the Great Lakes region, the three situations where we encounter steelhead in summer are also as varied. They range from small roll casts on Indiana's "spring creeks"—drainage ditches really—to classic steelhead rivers in all their summer vibrancy, to June's spawning steelhead in the natural spillway of the world's largest freshwater lake.

First let's go to Indiana where the Skamania steelhead were introduced in Great Lakes tributaries. It is not the prettiest place on earth, but I'm not the prettiest angler either . . .

Though I fly fish for summer steelhead in the spirit of Papa Hemingway, my pursuit often resembles the antics of Wile E. Coyote. It's the steelhead's fault, really. They have no sense of fair play. They can reject the best looking, most well-presented flies. When hooked they fight with the strength and agility of a gymnast. But the adventure is worth it, because the

spirit of Hemingway can arrive at the river, unless Bob and Lars show up first.

Bob Pieszchalla, Lars Rishaug and I, outfitted in waders, fly vests and polarized glasses, wove our way through the dense brush along Trail Creek, a tributary of Lake Michigan. The heavy foliage muffled the noise of Michigan City, Indiana. A warm late July rain tinted the gurgling creek. We knew summer-run steelhead swam in these waters, in a greater concentration than any other Lake Michigan tributary. Flyrods were our weapons of choice.

Well, for two of us at least. Lars had caught many steelhead but never on a flyrod. "I hooked one here on a Black Stonefly," Lars told Bob as he pointed at me. "But the Nimble Netter there didn't get it netted."

Bob glanced suspiciously at me.

"I *really* tried," I said lamely.

"I think I'll fish here," Bob said pointing at a pool. He slid down the three-foot high bank and stripped the line from his fly reel.

"Where are you going to fish, Lars?" I quizzed as he wove through the brush.

43

"I'm fishing under the logs around the next bend," Lars said without missing a step. "They like to hide under there."

"If you get one on, holler and I'll come running with the net," I said, as I swung the landing net like a kid catching a pop-fly.

"If I get one on, you'll be the *last* to know," Lars jabbed with a smile. "I see Bob brought his own net! Though I'm sure that's no reflection on you."

He laughed as he disappeared into the foliage. As Bob began casting, a steelhead porpoised in front of him and my preparation became more urgent. I tied 6-pound tippet and a number 6 Woolly Bugger. Of course, I began scanning the water for any sign of steelhead. I'd try staying between Bob and Lars—in case they needed my help netting a fish. Down the creek 100 feet I saw a shadow moving upstream. It kept moving upstream, then paused in the current. The steelhead was exposed and skittish. I was now within its 30-foot sight range and only heavy brush concealed me. The sole casting lane was a small opening between the trees less than 20-feet from the steelhead. So I crawled in the sand and knelt on the four-foot high bank; the fish was unspooked. I tried to cast upstream of the fish. My first cast caught in the tree to my left. The second caught in the tree on my right. The third cast caught in the left tree again. I was yet to get the fly into the water and had spent seven minutes carefully extracting my fly from the branches, while under the watchful eye of a wary steelhead. Wile E.'s paw prints were evident in the sand. After several more fruitless casts, I finally hit the water! But the fly was too short.

For the next twenty minutes I knelt, cast, changed flies, and alternated between extracting flies from trees and watching the steelhead reject my offerings. Finally, after I lightened my tippet to 4-pound test and tied on a

Lars on Trail Creek in Indiana

number 10 Green Caddis fly, I saw the steelhead's mouth open. I set the hook, slapping the rod against the brush, but missed the fish. It had spit out the fly. Excited by success I cast again. He took it. I missed. *I'll set the next one quicker*, I thought. In my rush to cast I tangled the line in a tree. The following cast went well—the steelhead struck, so did I. It was on. Hemingway cheered. I tried to leap to my feet, my left foot was asleep! Wile E. was nearby. The steelhead leaped and somersaulted then swam downstream toward some logs. With the reel screaming its protest, I slid down the bank as the steelhead jumped again. Just as I thought I might land the fish, it swam under a log and it was gone.

The line had broken. There would be more—reluctant steelhead, broken lines, straightened hooks, and lost fish.

We found in late summer the steelhead fight and jump like no other steelhead and salmon we chase. Both Lars and Bob outfished me that day, each hooking 10 or 12 fish—I hooked six.

Hooking these reluctant migrants was tough but netting them in these small creeks was even tougher. We found the summer steelhead schooling in pools and below rocky water falls. The small "natural" flies got the most strikes: small black stone flies, Hare's Ear Nymphs, Woolly Buggers, Green Caddis flies, and tiny egg patterns.

One steelhead kept emerging from under some overhanging brush to strike at something on the surface. It hit a black Marabou Muddler Minnow that I skated on the surface in front of it, but I lost that fish as well. The strikes were not arm jerking snaps but very subtle takes; often only a pause in the line's drift indicated a strike. But there was nothing subtle in the steelhead's reaction once we hooked them.

The high water-temperature of Trail Creek in July and August increased their metabolism like a shot of adrenaline. Every steelhead we hooked that day jumped at least once. Most jumped several times. They would twist in the air, hit the water and dart upstream and jump again. By mid-afternoon we were all fishing within sight of each other. Bob and Lars hooked fish regularly and I stayed between them with the net. We landed few fish and my reputation as the nimble netter was unimproved.

Somehow I knew my time of redemption would come. By late afternoon, Bob was still fishing his favorite pool. It seemed to boil with steelhead. When Bob cheered again, "Fish on!" I jumped into the stream. The steelhead somersaulted within five feet of me, but the water was too dark to see the fish. By the line we could tell that it now swam in front of Lars. Bob pressured it harder and it leaped again. Then Bob's line went limp.

"Is he off?" I asked.

"I'm not sure," Bob said, quickly reeling. "There—he was just swimming at me!"

When the line snapped tight to the steelhead it leaped again. It was close to the opposite bank when it leaped.

"Wow," Lars yelled. "Did you see that? That fish landed up on that two-foot high bank!"

As soon as it hit the bank it flipped itself off and back into the water. Then the line snapped.

"That one was not my fault . . ." I defended myself.

"I'm not so sure," Lars countered.

"Every dog has his day . . ." I rebuffed, wondering if coyotes had *their* day.

As Bob tied yet another fly to his tippet, Lars began casting and I waded back to pick my rod from a bush. As I untangled my line from the branches, Lars hollered. I tossed the rod into the bush again and grabbed the net. As I turned the fly line streaked past me.

> *Allow great care when fighting and landing summer acrobats. The warm water makes them more sensitive to fatigue*

"It's a strong one," Lars said as the fish swam upstream near Bob. It then swam onto the sand bar where Bob stood in a couple inches of water. Bob jabbed his net at it, guessing what direction it might go.

"That's a huge male," Bob said as it eluded him and disappeared into the stream.

"It's coming back," Lars said as I stood in the middle of the creek. I had the net level in front of me eight inches above the water. Suddenly the steelhead leaped out of the water and did a half gainer into my unmoved net.

"I did it!" I yelled.

Bob and Lars were both doubled over—laughing. "You see that, Lars?" I cheered looking over my shoulder at him. Then I felt the huge steelhead jerk. When I looked back . . . he was gone. The net was empty.

And I could almost hear a coyote howl.

Summer Runs In Small Creeks

Though the small Indiana creeks have tremendous runs of summer-run steelhead in July and August, they are tough to fish. If it rains an inch or so, the creeks are unfishable for nearly a week because of the muddy conditions. When they are fishable, they are like small Brookie creeks; casting is tough but the numbers and accessibility of steelhead make the effort and frustration worth it.

As we found repeatedly, the nymphs and tiny eggs produced the most strikes. The steelhead hold in the deepest pools—which would not even be called pools in most rivers—and the steelhead are often porpoising and playing. If you get into fresh fish from the lake—you usually fish within a mile of Lake Michigan—these happy fish will strike any fly that comes along. However, they are difficult to land because the narrow creek contains many downed trees and submerged logs.

The fish also hold in pockets below several small rock dams that exist on the creeks. I always fish these even if there is no indication of fish activity.

Unfortunately, the fish in these small creeks do not stay happy as long as fish in larger rivers. The creek warms up quickly in the hot July and August weather. On these small accessible creeks, high water temperature and intense angler pressure quickly sours their happy attitude.

Allow great care when fighting and landing these summer acrobats. The warm—at times hot—water makes them more sensitive to fatigue. Sometimes we could not revive a fish that we had caught. This is a sad aspect of this fishery.

Indiana also currently has special regulations on these streams that restrict anglers to using one fly (or hook) and a maximum hook gap. This is their response to the snagging and foul-hooking that plague these tiny streams.

Summer Runs on Larger Rivers

With the expanded Skamania steelhead plants throughout the Great Lakes region, more rivers now receive summer runs of steelhead. Coinciding with this expansion, trout fishermen are getting an unexpected response to their flies and more steelheaders are targeting these summer steelhead.

The sidebar on summer steelhead attitudes shows that summer run fish may be the happiest of all the steelhead we chased in Great Lakes tributaries. It is also the season of the year when there are the fewest fish in the river. However, the highest percentage of fish you will encounter will be happy, willing and ready to strike a fly. *Finding* these willing fish can be the problem.

There are three methods for finding the summer fish holding spots: the first is knowing the river and what types of pools and runs the summer fish hold. The second is finding where the ground water springs enter the river's current flow. The third is searching the runs and pools with streamers until you find a pod of summer fish.

When summer steelhead migrate into the river they will congregate for two reasons—the natural structure of the river and high water temperatures. Migrating fish will congre-

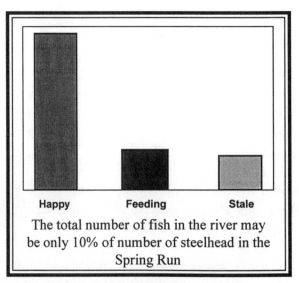

| Happy | Feeding | Stale |

The total number of fish in the river may be only 10% of number of steelhead in the Spring Run

Summer Run Steelhead Attitudes

gate in natural holds, like the pools below or above long shallow stretches of the river. Fish resist crossing a long shallow stretch because it exposes them to predators. The fish are also eager to rest once they swim through such a stretch. Dams present an obvious congregation area, even if they have a fish ladder.

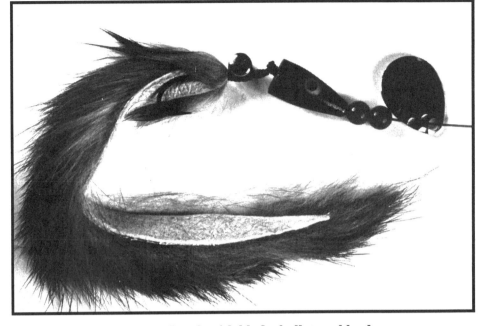

Bunny Strip Leech with blade, bullet, and lead eyes

When hot weather increases the water temperatures, the summer run steelhead seek the coolest water in the stream. You will find them in the deepest pools, especially in areas of the river where ground water springs enter the river's flow. Once the water cools, the fish could be anywhere in the river. You must search every likely run and cover lots of water with streamer flies to find the fish.

A hard time to fish in summer is when the steelhead move into the deep pools because of warm water temperatures. Then it is best to fish them at daybreak and dusk. The fish will not strike in summer pools at noon in bright light and 62° water temperatures. If you fish only between eleven and four o'clock in the summer you would swear that there are not any steelhead in the river.

To find steelhead by swinging streamers through the pools, use lead-eye Woolly Buggers in different colors. Use visibility to excite the fish. In the big pools it often takes lots of movement to attract attention to the fly, so try a number 6 up to 1-O Woolly Bugger.

According to Jim Johnson, "The highest percentage summer fly that I have used is a 5-inch strip of rabbit fur, which undulates and swims like a snake. For summer, I think the action is more important than the color—like fishing a Rapala lure."

The bunny strip fly is a 5-inch Zonker strip tied onto a hook but *not* wrapped around the hook shank. The strip undulates free in the current. Tie the rabbit strip to the hook and tie the monofilament to the shank then dangle a second hook three-quarters of the way back on the rabbit strip. With the second hook's position the fly gets more hookups per strike, because it catches more fish that "strike short." If the special regulations of your river prohibit two hooks, then cut off the first hook at the bend.

Hex-nymphs and egg flies are very effective patterns for summer steelhead in these larger rivers. Big gaudy streamers work best for searching the river for pods of fresh steelhead. Once you find a pod, stop and fish them with nymphs and eggs through the run.

"My personal choice for a gaudy streamer is made by putting two beads and a Colorado spinner blade on in front of the streamer," Jim Johnson said. "I cast this flashy pattern until I locate a pod of fish, by seeing a chase or a roll or some other fish activity. Then we stop and use a food item imitation and we can catch a higher percentage of the fish we found. Nothing locates the summer fish better than a fly with color, flash and lots of movement."

Techniques for Summer Steelhead

Every fly fishing technique takes fish in summer by swinging flies through pools. Shooting lines, sinktips, floating lines and full-sinking lines all work well. "But you still catch more fish if you keep the fly line away from the fish," Jim Johnson told me. "You read to the contrary all the time, but it is not true. Even in Alaska where the fish rarely see fishers, a fly line swinging through a pool will put the fish off the bite. I often fish a pool after a boat has fished a run with sinking line and cannot get any more strikes. I put on a floating line or a shooting line with a very long leader and put the weight in the fly instead of spread out throughout the fly line—my personal choice is lead-eyes—and start catching fish again in that run. I have done it time and again. So have my friends who fish Alaska.

"They have found that when Silver salmon get persnickety, if they switch to floating line with a long leader and a lead-eye fly, they start catching fish again. Use a fairly light floating line like a 3-weight weight-forward line (on a 5 or 6-weight rod) and let the weight of the fly make up the difference in the casting. I especially like Mono-Core fly line for this. I also fish with a Diarichi shooting line with only the lead eyes of the fly. Joe Humpheries did the same thing in the Pere Marquette 'One Fly Contest' and fished it with a leaded Sculpin pattern.

"In Arkansas, we fish with a 5-weight trout rod, Diarichi shooting line and a little lead-eye streamer and 10-12 foot tapered leader," Johnson continued. "You have to get some tip speed to cast it, and cast it around to the side. When I had to get a summer steelhead for photos in a newspaper article, that was how I fished. You can dead-drift it, shoot it, cast it. If you have brush behind you, you can strip it all in and shoot it out. I used to color-code the lead-eyes so I knew which weight I was fishing. But it was hard to keep all the selection I needed and in the colors I needed on a particular day. I now carry bass-worm bullet-sinkers painted black, in four sizes—1/64, 1/32, 1/16, and 1/8-ounce—and I slide them on the leader ahead of the fly. I still put the lead-eyes on the fly for effect, and the black bullet head snubs right up to the nose of a black Woolly Bugger. For a few bucks at the local fishing shop, you can have a season-long selection of weights for your streamers. You can fish any run you want by adding some different bullet weights. They make them in all colors. One June we hooked a big steelhead out of Canada Hole on the St. Mary's Rapids when I put a

Sault fishing in June

bullet and spinner blade on the front of a Woolly Bugger."

In the summer run the steelhead have a greater tendency to feed and chase. Most of the fish will be happy until they reach the heavily fished stretches of the river. Then you need to fish them more like harassed fish by nymphing for them with thin tippets.

Fishing Summer Runs

The biggest difference in summer fishing, as opposed to fishing redds, is that you are fishing an *area* instead of specific fish. Instead of targeting the nose of the steelhead, you fish an area and try to get the longest drag-free drift as possible. The fish could be anywhere in the run, so you must keep your flies in the strike zone for the longest possible time.

First try to cast as far upstream as you possibly can and control the drift as the flies come down past you. Then you mend the line as much as you can. You want to have 20 to 30 feet of drag-free drift if possible. This maximizes the time that the flies are near the bottom and in the strike zone. Then a long rod becomes more important, and the longer and lighter butt section of the tippet is crucial. When you are casting 45° upriver and drifting down to 45° downriver there is more line in the water and a much greater chance for drag to ruin the drift. The long, thin tippet may only get you an extra couple feet of the drag-free drift. After a thousand casts, it adds up to a tremendous amount of fishing—and catching.

Also, fish the pools with a little heavier Slinky than you would normally use, which will get the flies down more quickly. Then try to walk the weight through the first half of the drift by keeping the rod high. When the flies pass you, start to drop the rod tip and feed the line down to keep the weight from dragging the flies toward you. Let the weight drift as far downriver as possible before it gets swept to the side because of the pull of the fly line.

Since you do not know exactly where the fish are, you want to fish all the run. These fish are less likely to strike as a protective instinct and more likely to be feeding on natural food items. Fish with at least one "food item" fly, and most of the time two food items. At least one fly should have some action too, such as a Sparrow nymph, Hex nymph or a soft hackle Caddis Larva. Yarn flies also imitate egg food, and the fluorescent yarn holds its color even in the deep pool.

> *The biggest difference in summer fishing, as opposed to fishing redds, is that you are fishing an area instead of specific fish*

I have the poorest success for steelhead in pools over ten feet deep. They are always my last choice to fish. The only time I fish pools is when the temperatures are marginal. In the deep pools the current moves more slowly and the fish have a longer time to determine if the fly is a fake. In the swift current of redds and runs that is not so; the fish have to make a quick determination. Pools are a bait fisherman's domain, they outfish fly fishermen in pools and we outfish them in redds and runs. We cannot compete well in pools, because sight and smell become so important there.

In very warm water conditions a high percentage of steelhead congregates in the pools; then pool fishing becomes one of our only options. If the summer water temperatures begin to reach 60 to 62°, the fish go into deep pools. Fishing will be much tougher; it requires much longer and lighter leaders and very little weight. Pools have many little side eddies and billows that go up and down and sideways. There is not just a movement of water down through a pool. If your weight is going down though the middle, your flies may be moving up and across in an eddy. It takes a long leader to let the flies look natural, spend time in those areas, and attract strikes. So use as light as tippet as you can possible land fish on. Four and five pound is the maximum and you will get many more strikes on two and four.

June Spawning Steelhead

The third unique summer steelhead opportunity is the steelhead that spawn in June. Many Great Lake tributaries, which have a long natural history of spring steelhead migration, will have some fresh steelhead digging gravel in June. Ontario's St. Mary's Rapids has some of its strongest spawning during June. This results from the uniqueness of the St. Mary's waterway. The St. Mary's is the boundary water between Sault Ste. Marie, Michigan and its sister city of the same name in Ontario, Canada. The Rapids have a long history that includes details of the Native Americans using long handled nets from birch bark canoes to catch whitefish. Ernest Hemingway wrote for the *Toronto Star* that the St. Mary's Rapids was "the best rainbow [steelhead] fishing in all the world."

One unique trait of the Rapids is that it is the natural spillway of the largest freshwater lake in the world—Lake Superior. Lake Superior's cold water is literally legendary. That same cold water keeps the Rapids much colder, for a much longer time, than all the rest of the Great Lakes tributaries. It is also extremely clear water. I warn anglers continually, "If you look into a run and can tell that the water has even a *hint* of green, the water is over your head." The water is that clear. In St. Mary's the current is so powerful it scours the rocks and makes for treacherous wading in locations.

This river is almost the direct contrast to the Indiana creeks we began discussing. The Rapids area is a half mile wide and two-thirds of a mile long. The only similarity it has to Indiana's creeks is the civilization nearby. Sluice gates at the top of the Rapids control the flow of water that is regulated by the water diverted to the United States and Canadian hydroelectric plants and for the Sault Locks.

Another aspect that forces back the steelhead spawning time is the ice pack that flows downriver from Lake Superior and stacks up on the sluice gates. This chills the water. It is not unusual on May 9—when most steelhead rivers have already past their peak—that the ice pack still exists above the gates and the water temperature in the Rapids is thirty-nine degrees. Forty-two degrees is the major beginning of steelhead spawning, which in the St. Mary's is still a couple weeks away.

For several years before we moved to Sault Ste. Marie, my two sons and I made annual pilgrimages there to fish for steelhead after school finished in June. My oldest son, Micaiah, hooked a 12-pound hen steelhead (a fat, thick fish that looked like a Kaloop rainbow) on an olive and white Bunny Leech and landed her from the Rapids when he was only thirteen years old. That is not to say that fishing during June is easy—it can be anything but. Yet it can provide for some terrific fishing when the weather is warm.

During June the Atlantic salmon and some summer run Chinook salmon also enter the Rapids. While fishing a deep run, I hooked a fish that leaped like Atlantics I had caught elsewhere. It leaped at least ten times while streaking downriver into a deep pool. Then it surfaced and leaped a couple more times. I thought it was the largest Atlantic I had ever caught. But it turned out to be a male steelhead that I had hooked in the tongue. That hurts just thinking about it. I guess his tongue pain is what caused his leaping hysteria.

The summer run steelhead fishing can be a comical combination of Wile E. Coyote and Ernest Hemingway, but it is also filled with some hot steelhead action when we find those happy fish ready and willing to bite a fly. With cooler weather comes the salmon and the aggressive fall run of steelhead that follow them.

We will pursue them next . . .

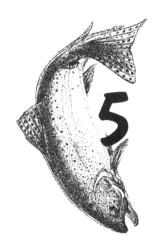

Fall Steelhead and
Some Atlantic Salmon

Targeting steelhead in September and October can become difficult because of the swarm of salmon that choke the rivers. But the steelhead do come in and dine on the eggs of the salmon, and the fall steelhead are eager to take a fly. They are fresh and strong from their pasturing in the big lake.

One fall day we found a pod of steelhead resting in a pool on their journey upriver. The pool was on a large bend in the river, and had a long shallow run above and below it. Some salmon schooled around with them and we hoped that we may bump into a lake-run Brown trout or two as well. Brown trout had surprised us in this pool before. The bright afternoon sun drove all the fish into the dark pools. I fished the head of the pool and John fished its tailout. We had several strikes at first, and landed some King salmon on olive Woolly Buggers and Egg Clusters flies. But soon the fishing slowed and we still had not hooked any steelhead.

After some time without a strike we changed to nymphs but received no response. Finally, John Silvas walked back to the boat for a pop and a snack. When he walked into the shallow water by the boat, he looked down at his waders and hollered, "Hey Kenn, look at this! I have Caddis larva clinging to my waders."

I walked on to the sand bar and my waders had dozens of Caddis on them. "Wow, that's a lot of Caddis," I exclaimed. "Have you tried any olive Caddis Larva yet today?"

"No," John said.

"Neither have I. But that's about to change," I said, as I pulled my fly box and knot tyer from my vest.

Moments later I had rerigged with a P.M. Hex-nymph and a Number 10 olive Caddis Larva on as the point fly. I was using 6-pound test line, so I tied the Caddis Larva on with an open-loop Rapala knot (see graphic on page 54). The open-loop knot allowed the small fly to dangle more freely and naturally from the heavy 6-pound test monofilament.

My first cast was a poor one, and the fish never saw the flies. My second and third casts also went astray. The fourth cast dropped the flies right into the lane where we had caught the salmon earlier. Less then a third of the way through the drift the fly line paused and I set the hook. As the rod swept back to my left and low to the river, I felt the resistance from a fish. I thought it was just another King, but wondered why they would take a Caddis. An instant later a bright fall steelhead thrashed to the surface, leaping and shaking its head.

"That's a steelhead!" John yelled. "A nice one, too."

> **It takes four or five days of high, warm water to bring the fall steelhead in good numbers**

We shared several moments of anxiety during the battle but finally the hen steelhead weakened and John netted her. After taking a few minutes to revive and release her, I celebrated the success with a Diet Pepsi and a smoked turkey sandwich on homemade French bread. But John was busy casting two Caddis flies into the pool. His efforts were rewarded, as were mine when I began fishing again. We hooked more steelhead and King salmon. Late in the afternoon, I hooked what I thought at first was a "jack" King salmon. Even before John netted it he knew it was a lake-run Brown trout that weighed about five pounds.

All that on one fall afternoon on the river—a sunny day, with a warm breeze, and active fish. How different it would have been if John had not noticed the Caddis on his waders.

The Fall Steelhead Run

Good numbers of steelhead enter the rivers each September but the King salmon are often so thick they make steelhead hard to target. The fall steelhead run seems completely dependant on high water flowing out to the big

lake. In 1986, for instance, a big flood hit in the second week of September. By the end of September many fall steelhead had migrated to the river.

In 1985, which many consider as the best fall run ever on the East shore of Lake Michigan, very high water existed for ten days during the end of September and into October. Before the river went down, on October fifth through seventh, the rivers were full of fall steelhead. Without those high water periods in late September and early October, the fish don't seem to come up until November or even the middle of the winter.

It takes four or five days of high, warm water to bring the fall steelhead in good numbers. Even if the high water comes too early, the fall run still comes into the river. Ideally, high water comes in the first two weeks of October, then the rivers get the best possible run. Though even in September high water will bring on the fall run.

"Most people feel that eliminating the peaking operation on Michigan's Big Manistee river has diminished the fall run of steelhead," Jim Johnson said. "They think that those small floods created the sensation of high water that motivated the fall steelhead to move upriver. I am not sure if that is fact or not. It is not clear whether the fish are in the river and move up more quickly because of the high water or if they come into the river *because* of the flooding."

Clearly the fall fish must have high water to motivate them into the upper stretches of these tributaries where most people are fishing them. High water brings the fish up into the faster sections of the river, and out of the slower marshy waters near the big lakes. The fish do not tend to concentrate into pods until they get upstream of these areas and get to a dam or rapids area.

November is traditionally *the* fall steelhead month. The older steelheaders say you can set your clock by November fifth. The late Aims

Steelhead hiding behind a rock in current

Finding Fall Steelhead

You rarely have difficulty getting fall fish to take a fly, it is *finding them* that is hard. The secret to fall fishing is to find the types of water that concentrate the fish. The top three considerations when looking for fall steelhead are: food (unless water temperatures become critical), then ground water springs, and then resting/staging areas (or pools below dams).

The fall steelhead seek out concentrations of food. They find where salmon eggs congregate, such as eddies full of eggs. When the salmon dig their redds they kick loose lots of insects—nymphs and Caddis larva. Fall steelhead relish these as well.

In the fall, if fish are in the river when the salmon are spawning there is only one combination of flies to use for fall steelhead—an egg pattern fly and a Caddis Larva. Pobst's study showed that eggs and Caddis must be ninety percent of the total diet of steelhead. In October and early November, many rivers still have a decent amount of Chinook and Coho salmon still digging up gravel until Christmas. Rivers like Michigan's Little Manistee, the Platt and the Big Manistee get good runs of Coho. Those rivers get so much Coho, anglers can depend on enough spawning salmon to get the fall steelhead to hold below them and take their eggs.

Borsum at Ed's Sports Shop in Baldwin, Michigan said, "You can count on one hand the number of years we have had a great fall run steelhead fishing before November fifth on the Pere Marquette." His experience reached back thirty years. Borsum fished several days a week in the fall for steelhead, and he considered November fifth through Thanksgiving to be the best time. Then he fished into the first or second week of December every weekday.

The Big Manistee is a much shorter river because it is only 30 miles from Lake Michigan instead of 80 miles like the Pere Marquette. The Manistee River tends to get steelhead a couple of weeks before November fifth.

"The fall fishing is very different from the spring. You likely will have ten to fifteen percent of the annual come run up in the fall," Jim Johnson said. "A couple thousand fish is a strong run in the fall for most Great Lakes tributaries. It is high quality fishing and the fish are more aggressive and jump better, fight better, and eat flies better. But you must search more for fish than in the spring, when you know where the fish are. Often the challenge in spring is getting visible fish to take, while in the fall it is to *find* a concentration of fish."

> *The top three considerations when looking for fall steelhead are: food, then ground water springs, and then resting/staging areas*

"Lake trout and Brown trout also spawn during that time of year and the fall steelhead will eat their eggs, too," Jim Johnson said. "In the fall of 1994, there were locals who fished the Manistee for decades and never caught a Lake trout until 1994. Then they were catching twenty Lake trout a day. Lots of Lakers spawned there in the end of October and early November. Maybe it is because there is no more snagging."

That year many steelhead held below the redds of Lakers and Chinook. Fishermen saw four or five steelhead holding below the redds taking eggs. These steelhead became very selective as to the type of egg fly they would take; they were very hard to fool. The fly fishermen tied small realistic eggs and used very light tippet to catch them. But eggs were the food that concentrated the steelhead there.

Obviously, a dam concentrates the migrating steelhead as well. Since there are relatively few fall steelhead per mile of river, it is difficult to fish blindly and randomly in dark deep water and expect to catch steelhead. You must find places and things that concentrate the fish. On most rivers anglers find fall steelhead at either ground water springs or food concentrations—not unlike the summer fish. Fall steelhead also hold in pools and runs above and below long shallow stretches, where they stop and rest on their migration.

"In my view, that is the secret of the Pere Marquette's First Clay Bank. It sits above a long shallow and below another long shallow and it stops fish both ways—below and above it," Jim Johnson said. "Burnt Cottage, up above, is the same thing. They have to run the long shallow and then there is another one in front of them as they come out of it. They wait in the deep

water before making another run through shallow water."

In fall the largest percentage of fish are feeding. The second largest percentage are happy fish. The minority attitude on the river is

Caddis Larva with soft hackle and tied with a Rapala knot

the stale fish. See the chart on the relative percentages of these three attitudes (page 56).

Like the day when the Caddis larva were clinging to our waders, we found that fall steelhead could be selective and specific to the food items adrift with the current. Learning that and casting food item imitations changed the complexion of our whole fishing expedition.

The Best of Times and the Worst of Times

The easiest time to find fall steelhead is not the easiest time to catch them. When a cold snap hits in the fall, the fall steelhead concentrate in the deep, slower pools. Because many rivers have few of these deep pools, locating the steelhead is easier. Amid a cold snap is the only time in fall when you will not quickly cover lots of water. Most fall days, you usually fish many lanes and cover lots of water. When the water temperatures fall below 40°, concentrate on the deep, slow water, and only fish three to five areas the whole day. Covering less water will not change your success that much; though the fish are slower and less aggressive, you have a better chance of finding them. During that time a place like the Pere Marquette's first Clay Bank Hole becomes almost a sure thing for a fish. You know there are always four or five fish there. But if the water temperature jumps up 10° and the water colors a little bit, those fish could be anywhere in the river. Then you start hitting every dark pocket along the way.

Searching Leaders

In the deep pools you may think that you should shorten your tippet, but the reverse is the case.

"The use of a long leader was taught to me by Dick Swan," Jim Johnson said. "Dick has had as much influence on fly fishing techniques in Michigan as anyone. He especially influenced me when I was young (sixteen or so) and I fished next to him several times by just running into him on the stream. I watched what he did, with his *searching leader,* that's the term he used, though he never described exactly what he meant by it. Here's what I can do with what I think Dick was talking about. A searching leader is at least a 10-foot tippet. Take an obstruction in a pool, like the huge rock in Oldie Hole. The average guy will fish down through there with a 18-inch tippet and will never get to the pile of fish laying behind the obstruction. The weight will pass on the near side of the obstruction and the flies will follow right with it and never get behind the rock to the fish.

"Often over the years, during the fall migration, we would come down to Oldie Hole and see the guys sitting on the bank. One day, like many others, I asked them how they are doing. They'd say something like, 'We hooked a few this morning but nothing since.' Now it's two in the afternoon, and they are all sit-

ting around on the bank. I asked, 'Do you mind if we try it?' They'd say, 'Oh no, go ahead, we're pretty much done here.' Or, they'd say, 'Okay, we're taking a break now.' Or sometimes, they'd say, 'Show us how to do it.'

"We pull the boat over and cut the rigs off and put on 10-foot of tippet and two flies. On the first cast, bang. Twenty fish later, those guys were ready to lynch us. For an hour and a half, we hooked fish on every third cast. We then say, 'Well, thanks a lot!' and move on downriver. Before we are around the bend they all jump up flogging the water with 18-inch tippets and never hook a fish."

> *Your strike percentage goes up if the fly always looks right, no matter how it flips around in the current. The best fly patterns cannot be upside-down*

The key is that huge rock that the fish get behind. You cannot get a normal drift into that spot. If you cast into the right place with a 10-foot (or longer) tippet, your weight goes down through. Then the flies on the long soft leader catch the eddy and the current. The weight has to be heavy enough to let the flies go down before the Slinky. As the weight finally gets down, the flies begin to swirl around in the eddy. Then the weight finally gets to the middle and the flies are still swirling. Finally the weight gets far enough below the flies that it begins pulling them out. The flies spend 20-feet of drift swirling and poking and searching around behind the debris and rocks. The flies can thus be presented to the fish that cannot ever be fished any other way.

On a smaller scale we do that with every fish in the stream. Every steelhead on the river will tuck into whatever cover it can find. A 18-inch leader will never catch fish behind even a small basketball-sized rock, because the fish has to dart out, grab the fly and dart back. If, however, you routinely tie on a 6 or 7-foot tippet the flies will tuck in behind even large rocks and lots of debris.

The long tippet drops the flies into any little depression, where steelhead hold to get a break from the current. Steelhead hold in eddies and swirls of current that the flies will not get into, unless you have a long enough tippet. When fishing redds, use long tippets to keep the weight—Slinky—out of the sight of the steelhead. In the pools, seeing the weight is less of a factor. The fish cannot see as well because of the dim light and the moving sand. In pools the sound and the visual aspects become less important. But the longer tippet remains important in pools to get the flies into cubby holes, eddies and behind obstructions, where the steelhead hide.

Flies for Fall Steelhead

In the fall, cast flies that represent food items while covering lots of water. Two egg patterns work well. Another great pair uses a bright fluorescent egg fly to attract the fish's attention from a greater distance; then a steelhead will notice a nymph fly. With the egg flies you still present a fairly realistic size and shape for a food item. A common fall rig is a char-

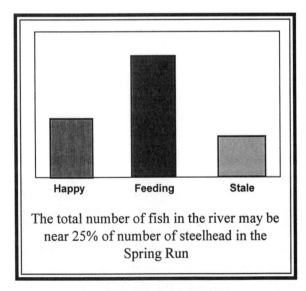

The total number of fish in the river may be near 25% of number of steelhead in the Spring Run

Fall Fish Attitudes

treuse egg as a dropper fly, and a natural egg for a "food item" as the point fly.

A high percentage of fall fish focus on food. For example, one fall Tom Johnson guided a fly fisherman who wanted to fish swinging streamers and dries for the fall steelhead. That year, 1991, the river was high and warm in November. Those were the best conditions for that fishing technique in the fall. November 5 was perfect: 50°, warm, high water. The anglers should have expected to hook several steelhead that day. These perfect conditions continued all that week. Tom's fisherman even raised a fish to a dry fly that week, but did not hook it. That whole week the fly fisherman swung Muddler Minnows and attractor streamers and only hooked two fish. His partner, who was Drift-fly-fishing with egg flies, hooked ten steelhead in the same period.

> *When fall steelhead target food, cast something that imitates what they are eating*

One fall, Tom and Jim Johnson and several fly fishing guides again confirmed the varying results of the different fly fishing techniques.

"One fall several of our guides and myself took some time off and went downriver. We cast big gaudy streamers and whatever we had," Jim Johnson said. "At one run, one guy fished through with swimming streamers, then the next one fished with a Teeny Line—he got the flies deep and mended the line. The third guy that came through fished two egg flies on a running line and hooked three fish out of a run. None of the rest of us had even gotten a touch, even while fishing techniques that should have worked. The run was not deep, we were getting down enough, but we were swinging streamers instead of imitation food. That young lad kicked our butts. We each got fish with the different methods, but the Drift-fly-fisherman took fish at will."

When fall steelhead target food, cast something that imitates what they are eating. Fall steelhead can become selective, not as much as Brown trout, but they will strike food flies first. If you cast something that is very different, you may catch some fish but not most of those feeding steelhead. Steelhead, like a Brown trout that is feeding on certain nymphs, will still

John Hunter in a "holding" pool

chase a Woolly Bugger that passes through. If a hatch is coming off and you are casting a Woolly Bugger to Brown trout, you will have a long day. If a steelhead finds a place to gorge on eggs drifting downriver, it will not move off that food line to chase a streamer that passes through. The steelhead will not waste time chasing something that might be food, by leaving a place it *knows* produces food. In those situations, you maximize your chances to catch fish by casting flies that imitate a food source with at least one of the flies. That is the beauty of fishing with two flies, you don't have to put all of your eggs in one basket.

"In the fall, I often use a #4 black Spey fly with a chartreuse butt and an egg fly," Jim Johnson said. "Black Bear Green Butt Skunk is a good fall steelhead fly. When I first started fishing, I had a lot of luck with that fly. It was basically a Spey fly with a black wing on it. I like a fly that can never be upside-down in the current—that is, a fly without a wing or a top."

If a fly has a wing, some percentage of time the fly must not look right, because it is not right-side-up. Your strike percentage goes up

if the fly always looks right, no matter how it tumbles or flips around in the current. The best fly patterns cannot be upside-down. Nymphs tied "in the round" are better than the ones with the top and bottom. Part of the Woolly Worm's success is that it has no top.

Obviously, flies like a Hex-nymph must have a top because of the nature of the nymph it imitates. But Sparrow nymphs, Woolly Buggers, Spey flies, Caddis Larva, and Egg flies are flies that cannot be flipped upside-down. If a fly looks upside-down only ten percent of the time, that is too often if you can avoid it. A wing on a fly also looks rigid in the water. A wing on a fly made of marabou or a rabbit strip adds life to the fly and minimizes the effect of appearing upside-down.

To make a fly ride a specific way, put lead-eyes on it. The lead-eyes make the hook ride up. Also, when you strip in the fly, the lead-eyes give it the up and down undulating action that excites the fall steelhead. By putting weight in the front of the fly—whether with lead-eyes or a bullet weight—the fly looks more alive and swims like a wounded minnow.

Fall may be the best time to take steelhead with strictly traditional fly fishing methods. Traditional techniques will never be the highest percentage method, but in the fall you can take steelhead that way, if your heart is set on it. Anglers have a good chance to catch fall steelhead on a floating line by swinging streamers though runs. Using strike indicators, nymphs, and eggs become effective because many fall fish actively feed. Traditional West Coast methods work much better in the fall than in winter or spring, but they may not work as well as they do in summer. However, on a warm fall day the West Coast techniques are not far behind the summer success rates.

A steelhead caught on an Atlantic Salmon fly by John Kilmer

"Remember the two anglers, where one hooked two fish with West Coast methods while his friend hooked ten by using the Drift-fly-fishing," Jim Johnson said. "Those percentages may be a good pattern. West Coast techniques will hook about 20 percent of the fish to Great Lakes techniques. Spey rods and big Spey flies and sinktip lines will have some reasonable success. Fall is a great time to experiment with such techniques."

Atlantic Salmon

Another fish we encounter in the fall is the migrating Atlantic Salmon. We encounter these planted salmon in three types of places—surf-fishing at the confluence of a river and lake, below dams and in big open rivers and rapids. Of all the fish we will talk about, the Atlantic Salmon have the most limited distribution throughout the Great Lakes. They have been planted in several locations but not as many, nor for as long, as the other salmon and the steelhead. Therefore, the opportunities for fly fishing for these classic fish are more limited.

When you find Atlantics, they are a treasure to catch. They are more like steelhead than their Pacific salmon cousins. The Atlantic salmon run upriver to spawn, then, like steelhead, return to the lake to wait for next year's migration. In the Great Lakes region we pursue Atlantic salmon in tributaries of the Great Lakes as well as those that are "landlocked" in smaller lakes.

On a fall day, John Silvas and I cast traditional Atlantic salmon flies at the confluence of a river—creek, really—that flowed into a lake. The Atlantics were schooling up at the mouth of the river to begin their spawning migration. It was particularly cold that fall day, and snowed before we finished.

We saw schools of Atlantics swarm into the confluence then swing back out into deeper water. We stood in waist deep water casting with traditional sinktip lines and Atlantic salmon patterns. As the day continued, other fly anglers came and fished awhile then left.

We would see an Atlantic porpoise, then cast ahead of where the school was swimming. We both caught Atlantics on traditional Atlantic Salmon patterns—especially the Eagle flies tied in yellow and black (the falconer in me comes out in everything). Catching an Atlantic on a traditional fly was my quest that day. I wondered if the other flies that I had found so successful on steelhead and Pacific salmon would work. So I tried several patterns such as the Hare's Ear nymphs, Stonefly nymphs, cream-colored latex wigglers, and Bunny Leeches.

> *The easiest time to find fall steelhead is not the easiest time to catch them*

When I switched to the other flies, the wind also switched and it began to snow. That was not a good sign. We did hook a few fish on nymphs and I caught my nicest male Atlantic salmon on a Number 4 olive Bunny Leech. He struck it with reckless abandon and leaped several times before Silvas could get him into the net. After a couple of quick photos we released him.

One odd characteristic we noted on our Atlantic trips was that the male Atlantics would burst onto the surface and skip along on their sides for as much as 15 or 20-feet before diving back under. These fish were not hooked or stung by a fisherman in any way. They would be swimming with the school in the confluence, then would inexplicably dart to the surface and bodysurf across for several yards.

The most telling time of one day came during a snowstorm just before dark. One small, well-bundled angler waded out into the confluence some distance from us and started casting without saying a word. We did not think anything of it, until the fisherman starting catching a fish from every school that passed. Our success had slowed late in the day. It was obvious to us that this was a local angler who knew this lake. After the angler released the third fish, we asked about the nature of the "secret fly." We received a pleasant surprise when we heard *her* voice. She was an excellent fly fisherwoman who felt free to share her success with us. She told us she was fishing a Number 14 Blue Winged Olive with the wings cut off, and fished it wet.

Great Lakes Atlantic Plantings—Mixed Success

Some Great Lakes states have attempted planting Atlantic salmon dating back as far as the 1920s, but success was limited. Once the Pacific salmon plantings resulted in successful natural runs on hundreds of Great Lakes tributaries, there was renewed interest in planting Atlantics. Historically, Atlantics were once found in the Great Lakes, mostly in Lake Ontario, but they disappeared shortly after the area was settled in the 1800s.

The results of Atlantic introductions throughout the Great Lakes states have been poor at best—a complete failure in some cases. The most successful plantings have been in inland lakes, but one unique waterway has had some success with Atlantics in the Great Lakes themselves. This is the St. Mary's River that connects Lake Superior and Lake Huron.

In 1987, Lake Superior State University, in Sault Ste. Marie, Michigan, started raising Atlantics in their aquatics laboratory in cooperation with the Edison Sault Electric Power plant. Their success has been encouraging. Now a predictable run of Atlantics can be expected to arrive in the lower St. Mary's River by mid-June. Then the Atlantics arrive at the Power plant and the St. Mary's Rapids by late June. Fly fishermen cast to Atlantics from boats tied to the exits of the Power plant, and in the Ontario side of the St. Mary's Rapids.

These Atlantics have been caught on classic Atlantic patterns, including the deer-hair Bombers flies. They are also caught by running Hex-nymphs and Caddis Larva flies deep in the runs and pools. The Rapids has an incredible hatch of *Hexigenia* mayflies and Caddis flies in the summer. One July day when we could not get the Atlantics to take any of the classic flies, we noticed all the Caddis flies that were hatching. I counted the sea gulls that were feeding on the Caddis hatch. There were over 250 sea gulls (in three groups) eating the Cad-

dis as they hatched. The gulls would fly upriver over a fast smooth stretch and land. As the powerful current pushed them downriver each gull would grab over 24 Caddis flies (I counted) before the next rapids forced them to fly back upriver. Each gull took about 35 seconds to complete a round trip. This spectacle continued for a couple hours. Literally, only the Lord knows, how many Caddis flies hatch in that Rapids each year. In July the Hex-nymph shucks we see in the Canadian Locks seem as numerous as the Caddis flies that day.

On the "Gull Caddis Day" we did not hook any Atlantics on traditional flies, so we changed to two Caddis Larva flies in different colors and hooked two fish and landed one.

If I had to choose between leaving home without an American Express Card or some green Caddis flies, it would be an easy call . . .

John Silvas with an Atlantic Salmon

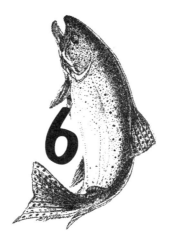

Winter Steelheading:

"A Chilling Anticipation"

Few events thrill steelheaders more than being at the right place at the right time. For most, steelhead fishing the "right time" means the prolific spring runs for steelhead that charge up the tributaries in search of spawning gravel. Who could argue with that? Anglers are now learning, however, that midwinter can be another right time on steelhead rivers. When steelheaders think of winter fishing, they envision hot-shoting—back-trolling with plugs—or drifting spawn bags through pools, but not fly fishing. That is all about to change. Fly fishing steelheaders need not hibernate in winter; they can and do catch steelhead in those frozen months.

The cold weather often drives fly fishermen like me from the streams to the fly tying benches. But once I have tied several dozen steelhead flies, created a couple new patterns and added new twists to favorite patterns, I get a very bad case of cabin fever.

My doctor, a fellow fisherman, said that the *only* prescription for a cure is "the real thing—fishing." I agreed. But what chance does a fly fisherman in the dead of winter have?

After a few calls to friends near my favorite steelhead rivers, I learned that in midwinter the steelhead still swim up the rivers whenever they get the urge and appropriate water conditions. The fall run of steelhead settle into the deepest pools and the early migrants for the spring run join them throughout the winter. Realizing this, I sat at my fly tying bench and pondered which pool would hold steelhead in this frigid weather. I remembered one winter trip when a friend and I fished a favorite pool, we hooked and netted a bright silver, male steelhead. After we took several pictures of it, a fly fishing guide drifted past with his clients.

"How is it going?" he asked.

"Great," we responded almost in unison.

"We just caught a chromer male from this

pool on a small Hex-nymph," I explained.

"Yes, that pool has produced steelhead for four straight days," he said.

"I've always liked this pool," I replied.

Years ago, I did not know *why* that pool was so productive, especially in winter. Thoughts like those rattle through my head every winter as I sit at my fly vise and watch the snow accumulate by the inches. Knowing that steelhead are out there and that they *can* be caught drives me out in the snow to prepare my driftboat and gear for yet another winter sortie after steelhead.

There are several reasons to leave the warm comforts of home to pursue winter steelhead.

Reasons to Chase Steelhead in Winter

Seven reasons urge me to risk cold, ice and frostbite to go winter steelheading. They are: a cure for cabin fever; the winter migration of steelhead into the river; the freshness of winter fish; the knowledge that steelhead congregate into very specific locations; the fact that very few anglers venture to the river in winter; and winter's unharassed steelhead that willingly take flies. Finally, winter can include some of the best steelhead fishing of the year.

Admittedly, the first reason, cabin fever, is more a response to the angler's mind-set than the river conditions. Ice fishing—especially with flies—is a real treat, and spearing pike and musky is akin to big game hunting. Still, I yearn for those moments when the river's current pushes against my waders and a bright steelhead thrashes on the end of my line.

Secondly, much of the year's steelhead migration enters the river during the winter months. As the winter run steelhead enter the river they can amount to 40% of the year's migration. More winter fish enter the river every time a meltoff occurs. Each time the river's flow increases, the steelhead migrate from the Great Lakes into the tributaries. These fish are unharassed and happy fish, though the frigid water they enter can often hamper their atti-

tude and actions. If you fish on the right winter day you can have a "hay day" without the hay fever.

Thirdly, many steelhead are very bright and silver because they recently left a Great Lake. Summer and fall run steelhead wear their spawning colors during the winter months. You may think that winter steelhead would not fight hard because of the frigid water, but that has not been my experience. The freezing water may hamper their energy but they are so fresh from the lake that I have a hard time noticing the difference.

> *As the winter run steelhead enter the river they can amount to 40% of the year's migration*

Fourthly, in winter the steelhead congregate in specific locations more consistently than at any other time of year. If you find a *hot* winter pool, it will often produce fish steadily in winter. In these cold water temperatures steelhead will always go to the warmest water in the river. As we will see, this is in three locations: deep pools, solar-heated shallow gravel-shelves, and wherever ground water springs enter the river's current flow.

The fifth reason I enjoy winter steelheading is the solitude. Generally it is only us and a guided trip on the river. Unlike any other season, winter provides the angler the pick of any pool or run. The crowds that storm the banks during April are elsewhere. Therefore the number of responsive fish compared to the number of fishermen is incredible compared to April's zoo.

That leads us to the sixth reason, because there are so few anglers, the only fisherman who can harass the steelhead is you. These unstressed and unhassled steelhead are willing to take a fly when it tumbles through the current in their direction.

My last reason is that winter steelheading can be some of the best fishing of the year. If an angler picks the day carefully and selects the pools and runs correctly, he cannot only cure cabin fever—which can be cured just by drifting down a steelhead river—he can have a day worth telling his grandkids about. And the walk through the seven-foot snow bank may not be an exaggeration!

Understanding the limitations and expectations of winter steelhead is the key to a successful and safe venture.

A Monthly Snowy Profile

The weather determines the winter steelheading situation more than any other single factor. When the cold weather arrives in earnest and the water temperatures keep dropping, then the fall season is over and winter fishing begins. Ordinarily the transition time from fall to winter steelheading happens in December. The air temperature drops, the snow begins falling and the happy and hungry fall steelhead turn into selective and reclusive winter steelhead. Those fish we pursued in the slots behind spawning salmon now seek out deep pools and the river's warmest water.

Winter Steelhead

> *Anyone who ventures out in January or February without a thermometer begs for failure*

If January produces a severe winter, the rivers can be frozen shut to any fishing except ice fishing. In the northern section of the Great Lakes tributaries this is usually the case, and they are typically frozen over. In the southern section the opposite is true; winter has to be ultra-severe before those rivers close completely. Great Lakes tributaries with dams, such as New York's Oswego and Salmon rivers, keep the water open all winter. The rivers in the mid-range of the Great Lakes tributaries vary the most from year to year. They can be frozen shut completely or can have spawning fish in January. That is quite a variety. But I have seen both on the same river a matter of twelve months.

February can be much like January in a harsh winter—especially early February. Fishing in early February in a bitter winter can be worse than January. By mid-February my cabin fever usually hits the worst and fortunately winter is usually releasing its grip on some rivers. With days where the air temperature rises and the sun, which is rising higher in the sky each day, hits the water in earnest, fishing success rises too. Successful fishing, like the weather, can be a roulette game any time during winter, but especially so in February. You want the weather to be warming but not too warm. If it gets too warm the snow will melt in abundance and the icy runoff will cool the river's temperature. This can shut off the fishing on a very warm February day. If the water temperature rises anywhere close to 45° Fahrenheit, some females will begin to spawn.

On some Great Lakes rivers this means winter spawning of Skamania steelhead or early spawning of the spring migration. These spawning events will happen generally on the rivers with a long history—several decades or more—of natural steelhead runs. March can be considered a part of the winter steelheading. Early March on bitter winters can be as tough fishing as February or even January. It too is affected by the depth of winter snow fall and the timing of the massive spring runoff. The fishing will get better and better as the month passes. Often March is my favorite time of the year. The April crowds have not arrived, the water temperatures are rising and the steelhead are becoming more active as the days pass. High, colored water can also provide some great fishing.

March is the transition month; by mid to late March it is no longer winter fishing at all. The water temperatures are quickly climbing to 45° and higher, so by the last week of March the spawning begins in earnest. Spawning is best between the third week of March through the third week in April. Northern Great Lakes tributaries are generally later and the southern tributaries can be sooner.

A Winter Trek

Armed with a thermometer, fly fishing gear, nymph flies, warm clothes, and proper technique, a steelhead angler can achieve more than just a day of solitude on the river. He can experience some excellent steelheading in January, February and especially into March. Winter steelhead fishing usually holds some surprises too. I have caught—and released—some

large Brown trout in January and February.

You may expect winter steelhead to be sluggish and unresponsive to flies. Yet in the right conditions and water temperatures, they strike nymphs, tiny eggs and even streamers with regularity.

Melting snow from two days of warmer weather trickled into the river. Birds chattered in the trees, but we knew this respite from winter's grip would be a short one. So we packed the driftboat. We cast in the gear, including

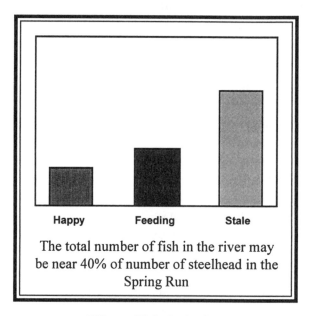

The total number of fish in the river may be near 40% of number of steelhead in the Spring Run

Winter Fish Attitudes

some dry clothes in the waterproof bag. We plucked some of our newly tied creations from the drying magnet at the fly bench, and headed off to the frigid river. It was mid-January. We knew that in winter there is no need to be on the river at dawn. Usually mid-afternoon fishing is the best, when the water temperatures rise as high as they will get that day.

As the afternoon sun crossed the sky, the fish became more active. The water temperature rose into the low forties. The steelhead began to move to the heads of the pools instead of holding in the pool's deepest slot. I even saw a Brown trout working two-foot-deep water over a gravel shelf; it may have been seeking out the water warmed by the gravel's solar-heating. I tied on two nymphs and cast through this run several times without a strike.

Often during those casts the trout would dart to one side of the other. Finally I wondered if he was darting after minnows. I tied on my smallest Muddler Minnow and a Hex-nymph. On the second cast I had a strike, but was so surprised that I missed setting the hook. On the fourth cast he struck again and I had him on the Muddler. He was a nice 15-inch Brown trout. On other winter days, I have taken and released trout on Hex-nymphs and Caddis nymphs.

> *Understanding the limitations and expectations of winter steelhead is the key to a successful and safe venture*

Though I caught some winter trout on streamers, the most productive steelhead flies are very tiny egg patterns and nymphs—Hex-nymphs, Caddis Larva, Hare's Ears, small Sparrows and tiny black stonefly nymphs.

Later that afternoon, we arrived at one of my favorite winter steelheading pools. Squirrel tracks dotted the snow between the trees on the tall bank opposite us and icicles, created by the melted snow, hung from the undercut bank across from us. The icicles reached down to the surface of the current and encircled the outer edge of the pool along this sweeping bend in the river. Upriver was a long shallow stretch of gravel that these steelhead would later use for spawning. From experience, I knew that a ground water spring entered the current's flow near the gravel shelf. The water temperature in this stretch was always warm in winter and cool in August. The towering bank on the opposite side often also indicated the presence of a ground water spring. Downriver from the pool was a gravel stretch, which made this pool a "resting area"

as well as a "staging area" for migrating steelhead. The pool was over eight feet deep and was the deepest pool in this stretch of river.

We preferred the *smallness* of this stretch of river because there is less current for the winter sun to warm. When we tested the water temperature, we found it was three degrees higher than any water upriver. The warmth was a combination of the sun heating the gravel above the pool and the nearby ground water springs.

We each tied on a number 10 black stonefly nymph and a Hex-nymph with 5-pound test tippet. John Kilmer, a professional fly tyer and my fishing partner, began casting at the head of the pool and I began fishing its tail. There was no wind and the bright winter sun warmed us through our layered clothes.

After every third or fourth cast we had to stop to melt or break the ice from our guides. It was a pain but worth the effort.

"Well, we could be at home or at the office," I said to John as we cleared our guides. "We sure wouldn't catch any steelhead if we were."

"This looks like the perfect pool to me, Kenn," John responded.

"It seems to have all the factors we need for good fishing," I commented as I changed Slinky Drifters. "I'm going lighter on my weight. I'm getting caught up a little at the back of this pool."

> *For winter steelheading one method is the most effective and productive: Drift-fly-fishing with Slinky Drifters*

John nodded and turned to cast again. I watched as his flies landed in the current next to the rugged logs of a manmade fish hide. He held his rod high as the flies disappeared into the flow. Then, just past half way through the drift, the fly line paused and by reflex or instinct John swept the rod downriver to set the hook. The line drew tight.

"You got one?" I hollered.

"It's not moving," John moaned, "Maybe it's that log again." He turned to me with a smirk, then he felt the first jerk. His look was one of surprise and delight as his rod was almost pulled from his hand.

"I *do* have one!" he cheered, as the reel began to sing—a pleasant sound in the dead of winter.

For the next several minutes John fought the steelhead in the pool; he was in no hurry to get the fish out. We knew from the fight that it was much heavier than the 5-pound-test line he fought it with. I grabbed the net from the boat and waded downriver onto the gravel shelf waiting for John to guide the fish out from the tail of the pool.

> *All these little things increase the percentages a small way, but they add up over a season*

Moments later, a bright male steelhead between seven and eight pounds was in the net. After much hand slapping, cheering and celebrating, I took my camera from the waterproof box and snapped several photos to capture the wintery moment. Then we took turns holding the steelhead in the current until we revived it enough to swim on its own. Once we released the fish, we returned to the side of the boat to light the propane *Mr. Heater* radiant heater. After a few more minutes, we had warmed our numb hands, dried our knit gloves, and heated up with a cup of hot tea. The cabin fever was then a distant memory.

We fished that pool and hooked three more steelhead before we moved downriver to find another ideal pool. That pool has always been a consistent producer, if the water temperatures cooperate.

Water Temperatures

Having the right flies is important to success for winter steelhead, but more important is water temperature. The swing in water temperature of the river is the single most important factor for winter fishing. Anyone who ventures out in January or February without a thermometer begs for failure.

In large part, a winter steelheader's "reading the river" means checking the water temperature at every bend and pool. Everyone knows steelhead respond differently as the water temperature varies—in water under 37° Fahrenheit, steelhead fishing will be slow or nonexistent. In most Midwest winters, the rivers in the middle sections of the Great Lakes region—like Michigan's AuSable, Pere Marquette and Manistee rivers—will only be below this water temperature one in three days. In the southernmost tributaries—especially in Ohio, Pennsylvania, lower Michigan, Illinois, New York, and lower Wisconsin, the percentage will be less than that. In upper Wisconsin, Minnesota, northern Ontario, and Upper Michigan—especially the tributaries of Lake Superior—the percentage will be constantly higher. Some weeks will be a total lockout because of the frigid air and water temperatures. I journey to the southern tributaries of the Great Lakes region to enjoy the best winter steelhead fishing.

> *A winter steelheader's "reading the river" means checking the water temperature at every bend and pool*

In 38 to 43° water, steelhead move to the head and tails of the pools, and some move into feeding stations. These temperatures produce fish, especially if the water temperatures are *rising* in the afternoon. Once the water temperatures climb to 44° and above, more steelhead move into feeding stations and winter steelheading begins in earnest.

Steelhead Response to Winter Water Temperatures

44 degrees F. and up	*Steelhead move into feeding stations; some move onto spawning gravel; many will take flies in runs near spawning areas*
38-43 degrees F.	*Steelhead move to heads and tails of pools, and a few move into feeding stations.*
Below 37 degrees F.	*Steelhead move into deep pools and their response is very slow or non-existent*

In February a swing in the water temperature—even as little as two or four degrees—will determine the difference between knocking them cold or just getting cold. On two days with the water temperatures of 42°, the fish can respond in the opposite manners. If the water temperature is 42° and it just rose from 38°, it's a boon—the fish are on! If the water temperature just dropped from 45° to 42°, it's a bust—the fish are off.

Water temperatures in midwinter are relative to what they were yesterday or a few hours ago. Steelhead strike more in the day's warmest water; therefore the hours after 2 P.M. provide the best winter angling. On sunny afternoons the water temperatures can rise two or three degrees, which can start a feeding spree not unlike that of midsummer when the water cools in late evening.

Finding the Ideal Winter Pool

For winter steelheading one method is the most effective and productive: Drift-fly-fishing with Slinky Drifters. Use a small Slinky and a long, light tippet. Winter steelheading is primarily pool fishing with realistic nymphs.

Several factors need to be sought out when selecting the ideal pool for winter steelheading. Those factors include: a stretch of river with the smaller amount of total current flow; the deepest pool in that stretch of river; a long shallow stretch above and/or below the pool; ground water springs entering the flow; and areas where the winter sun warms the gravel to solar heat the water.

In winter, try to fish areas that contain the least amount of river flow possible. Fish stretches of river upstream of where major tributaries enter the river. With the lighter volume of water, the air temperature and sun will have a greater impact on raising the temperature. If the water temperature is falling, fish a section with larger water flow because it will take longer for that section to cool. This will give you a larger window of time to catch fish before the dropping water temperature affects them.

Searching out the deepest pools in that stretch of river is effective because the deep pools often have the warmest water in the bottom, and will usually hold more fish. Seek out a pool with long shallow stretches above and/or below it. These long shallow stretches will concentrate the steelhead as they migrate up-river. This is not unlike seeking out the fall fish as they migrate. Winter fish often hold in the same resting and staging pools as the fall fish.

Winter fish instinctively find the warmest stretches of the river. The primary factor for creating the warmest water is the sections with ground water springs enter the current flow. These can be found by using a thermometer at every bend and pool of the river. They can also be found by testing water temperatures near areas where tall banks overshadow a gravel bottom in the river. These factors often signal the location of a ground water spring. Fish downriver of these springs and you will be rewarded for finding the warmest water in the river and consequently the most active steelhead.

Finally, the stretches with shallow water over gravel can be the warmer stretches in late afternoon on sunny days when the bright winter sun uses solar heating to warm the current. This slight increase in water temperature can mean the difference between a successful day of fishing and getting skunked. Also look where the winter sun warms the shallow, water (two to three feet deep) over a gravel shelf. In late winter, big brown trout move onto these sunny shelves (in water temperatures above 44°) to feed on minnows.

Also remember to seek out rivers that flow from large reservoirs where the water is freed from lower—and warmer—sections of the reservoir. The water of the reservoir stratifies in winter and the warmest water is lower in the lake.

If the dam frees water from the lower section—not from the spillway—this warmer water can create hot fishing action even on overcast, cold winter days.

Midwinter Flies

The drift-fishing technique is by far the most productive technique for winter fishing. It is never more true that you must present the flies into the nine-inch square "strike window," than in winter fishing. These winter fish will not journey far to strike a fly. You must go down after them, and Drift-fly-fishing is the best method to accomplish this. Though winter steelhead won't travel far for a meal, they will strike a nymph that drifts to them. Work each pool carefully as you fish downriver.

Productive midwinter flies are very realistic imitations of the natural insects in the river.

A tall bank over a gravel shelf can indicate a ground water spring

The flies must be more exacting in winter than any other time of year. Try to match the naturals in size, color and movement. Jointed Wiggle nymphs are one of the most effective patterns. These flies are tied in two sections—on two hooks—that are attached with monofilament. The monofilament allows the thorax section and the body section to move more naturally. Note though, the double hook flies are illegal in many "flies only" regulation waters. If you fish there just cut one hook off at the bend. The best patterns for winter Hex-nymphs are Tom Johnson's P.M. Wiggler or Oscar's Hex-nymph, which uses philoplume (the aftershaft of pheasant feathers) to imitate the gill-plates of the *Hexegenia* nymph. The orange thorax is also a key factor in the success of Oscar's fly.

> *Dressing for the cold and preparation for an untimely swim are necessities for winter steelheading*

Number 10 Black stonefly nymphs tied around the bend of a short shank number 8 hook is another very effective pattern for midwinter. The olive Caddis Larva fly with two turns of hackle at the collar and even the black Caddis fly (with a soft hackle collar) catch many fish in winter. The color of insect in the river you fish and the clarity of the current (because of the runoff) determine the colors of Stonefly nymph and Caddis fly. Small Gold-ribbed Hare's Ear nymphs are effective too, if tied in sizes 10 and 12.

While fishing deep pools with slow current, realistic flies are important because the fish get a long time to examine a fly before they take it. This means they have a much longer time to find something wrong with the fly's size, color, or movement.

Though streamers take steelhead during the winter, nymphs catch the most fish in the snowy months. For the Pere Marquette River, for ex-

ample, February and March generate heavy activity for three species of small, black stone flies, and a black Caddis fly. Black nymphs in sizes 14 to 8 cover the range for this season. As I mentioned, I tie a Number 10 fly on a short-shank number 8 hook. This nymph has proven very effective.

When a midwinter melt-off sends oxygen-poor water into the river system, *Hexagenia* (Hex) nymphs go into "free drift." This high, cold, dark water calls for careful wading, but a size 4, 6 or 8 realistic Hex-nymph will score highly—in fact, any other nymph will be ignored.

Dressing for the Cold

If winter steelhead fishing offers some unique rewards, it also has its dangers. Be careful wading, and keep your feet warm. Frostbite is a real danger when good fishing begs you to stay on the river, especially if you wear stocking-foot waders instead of boot-footed waders.

Obviously the greatest danger in winter steelheading is the cold. Frostbite on feet and hands is a real but manageable danger. The frozen banks and ice paths make falling and falling in more likely. Also the snow and ice often pack on the bottom of wader boots, especially on felt-bottomed boots, which makes for slick walking and wading. The cold air and water are hazardous to face and fingers.

> *Productive midwinter flies are very realistic imitations of the natural insects in the river. The flies must be more exacting in winter than any other time of year*

Dressing for the cold and preparation for an untimely swim are necessities for winter steelheading. The most urgent danger comes from spending hours in the frigid water while wading and fishing. So the best protection is the use of *boot*-footed neoprene waders. Boot-

Driftboat with Gear

to draw the water *into* your waders. Also, always carry an extra set of dry clothing and a warm winter coat in a waterproof bag in your driftboat or canoe.

Carry two or three pairs of wool-blend knit gloves. Neoprene gloves never keep my fingers warm. A long handled net also keeps your hands and arms out of the frigid water while landing fish. A brimmed, insulated hat with ear covers is a great blessing when a northwestern wind blows in.

Though I prefer no treatment on my fly line in winter, a spray fishing lubricant does help on the reels (applied at home) and for the rod guides (applied at the river). We have mentioned a good readable thermometer on a lanyard is a winter necessity.

A radiant propane heater also makes a winter trip more bearable. In my driftboat I take a heater attached to a 20-pound propane tank—be careful because it can quickly burn through tippets and fly lines. It will also melt some rain jackets.

footed waders—as opposed to the socking footed waders—are a necessity. The stocking-footed waders will not keep your feet warm for a day of winter fishing. Many anglers purchase their booted neoprene waders a size larger so they can put some extra warm socks inside. Using wool-blend socks that wick the moisture away from the skin work best. I prefer felt-bottomed waders but in winter it is best to use spiked-boot-soles attached to boot bottoms. This is the best protection against falling in.

Layer the warm clothes you wear on your chest. One unusual idea, which helps greatly, is to put your sweater *outside* your waders. If you keep it on the inside, it will act like a wick

When I walk into Ontario rivers in late winter, I fill a backpack with a Mr. Heater Jr. (or a fire starting kit), a compass, a thermo-blanket (which weighs only a couple ounces) and maps of the area. Ontario provides some great late winter action.

Winter steelheading will never exceed the popularity or productivity of the spring fishing, but anglers *can* catch steelhead in winter. In these cold months when April seems a millennium away, the right time to go fishing will be the next sunny winter afternoon.

Spring Steelheading

If the mystique of landing a steelhead rivals bagging a 10-point buck, how could two anglers—this side of the Pearly Gates—hook over 60 steelhead and land nearly twenty in one day? I will not tell you the number of strikes we had; if I did, it would sound like fishing spider flies over bluegill beds, not nymph flies to steelhead on redds.

So, how did we?

At first, one may wonder about a conspiracy between God, guide, steelhead, and the Michigan Travel Bureau. I resolved it was the insight and experience of Jim and Tom Johnson. Years ago, one drizzly, late-April day Jim Johnson and I fished the seven-mile "flies only" section of the Pere Marquette River. My guide and Jim's brother Tom coached me on my first Drift-fly-fishing adventure.

We began at Lumberjack Bend. There three steelhead flashed in the clear water rushing over a gravel shelf that has welcomed wild steelhead since the 1880s. The aggressive males battled for the right to create the next generation. A belted kingfisher scolded us from above.

We waded out a few feet from the drift-boat, concealing our silhouettes from the steelhead with the trees that lined the bank. I stripped fly line from the reel, then I aimed the cast 15 feet ahead of the fish. The flies dropped into the current when the line tightened against the reel.

"Keep your rod tip up high," Tom reminded me. "It keeps the belly from the line for more sensitivity and quicker hooksetting."

The Slinky drifter began ticking on the gravel as it passed me, seven feet above the fish. The current pushed the flies deeper each time the Slinky hit the bottom, bringing them into the steelhead's strike zone. I moved the rod tip parallel with the flies drifting downstream. Short thumps, with the rhythm of a human pulse, registered in my right hand.

"You won't feel a strike," Tom said. "Set the hook if you feel any pause."

A steelhead shook its head as its white mouth opened to dislodge the fly. I swept the rod low and downstream. Too late.

"Missed it, didn't I!"

"You sure did," Tom said patiently. "Cast to the same area. They often strike the fly twice."

The steelhead drifted back on the redd, closer to the deep run. So I moved downriver two steps and cast again. And again. Several casts later the rhythm paused and I set the hook with a sharp, downstream sweep of the rod.

The steelhead jerked its head against the tension, then panicked and rushed upstream.

"Get the line on the reel," Tom said. "Keep the rod low and to the side."

As I took up the line on the reel, the steelhead shot out of the water, turned, and streaked downriver. I followed, trying to keep enough of an angle to direct it a little. As I chased the steelhead around the first bend it ran toward one of those ever-present log jams. The steelhead stripped the line from the reel but failed to reach the logs, then turned downriver again. Past the second bend, it finally showed signs of tiring and Tom netted it.

As I held her, waiting for her strength to return, she glimmered in the current like polished silver, crowned with jade. Yellow sand framed her in gold.

A loud splash from upriver drew Tom to his feet. We knew they would visit us, if Jim kept the steelhead on.

"Is this normal?" I asked, wondering about our early success.

"Well, 75% of unspooked steelhead will strike a nymph. Hooking and landing the fish is another story," Tom answered. "Ten years ago most fishermen had not heard of using nymphs for steelhead fishing. Now nymphs account for three of four fish caught on the Pere

Marquette except during the fall Chinook spawning when egg flies produce best. Nymphs are effective all season for the same reason egg flies work well during the salmon run. The most effective flies imitate what is naturally drifting past the steelhead that day."

"The traditional bright streamers appeal to the aggressive, protective instinct of the steelhead," Jim continued. "But because steelhead feel out of their element in shallow water, they often leave the redd instead of striking the intruder. A number 2 chartreuse streamer scares most steelhead because it doesn't look like a forage fish after eggs, but like a foreign object in the stream."

"Steelhead see nothing unusual when a nymph drifts toward them on the current," Tom continued. "Nymphs call upon a different instinct with the steelhead-reflex. We make it easier for the steelhead to eat the nymph than move out of the way. But they take the flies so casually there is no strike to feel."

When my right hand felt the strength of the steelhead's tail, I released my grip. As she swam into the current I thought of the Apostle

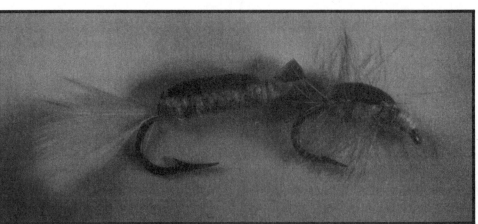

A "Jointed Wiggle Hex-nymph"

Peter releasing the fish that yielded the four-drachma coin. She was free, but I had the treasure.

Between three morning showers we fished our way downriver. At times the shallow water and tight contour demanded that we cast from our knees and scramble to our feet when a steelhead struck. On Doc's Bend I hooked and landed a 16-pound, 34-inch, red-streaked male on a Number 6 Hare's Ear Nymph. He was battle worn. We spent over an hour hooking, fighting, and photographing 7 to 16-pound steelhead on that series of redds.

> *The most effective fishing technique will trigger the passive-aggressive response from the steelhead*

By late morning when we reached the redds of Basswood, the sky cleared and the temperature climbed steadily until it peaked near 80°. Pine scent drifted across the river. With a rise in water temperature the steelhead fought vigorously. Of the 14 steelhead we hooked there, we—er, Jim—only landed one. The steelhead abused our hooks, tippets, rods, and reels with a leaping spree that rivaled any Olympic high-jump competition. One steelhead, as if trained at Sea World, evaded Jim by leaping out of the water and *over* a log. Other more traditional steelhead swam around submerged logs or broke lines with leaping head snaps. The steelhead charged anywhere they wanted on their first wild run. Like Jonah, we waited to see where the Great Fish would take us. There was no stopping them. Once I applied hand pressure to the reel, but the steelhead lunged and snapped the tippet. Tom just shook his head.

With this nymphing technique we hooked steelhead with such incredible consistency that I gave Tom the rod and held the camera in focus while he made each drift. When he set the hook, I paused, then snapped the shutter when the steelhead leaped.

We ate lunch while drifting between fishing spots to angling that was as fast and testing as the morning's. That Tuesday, Jim hooked 37 steelhead and landed 11, while I hooked 24 steelhead and landed eight. The percentages may not sound great, but remember we weren't fishing spider flies over bluegill beds.

Redd Techniques

Most of the fish we pursue in spring are stale because of the spawning season (*see page 79*). Therefore, spring techniques must account for targeting these stale fish. As we saw earlier, the most effective method will trigger the passive-aggressive response from the steelhead. We must sneak a fly down to the fish, then have it jump up and shout "Boo!" When it does, the stale fish will grab it like we swat away an ink pen that someone throws at us.

When fishing redds of steelhead, you can be successful with every type of fly fishing technique. Shallow redd fishing is the least discriminating of all fishing conditions. Here it matters the least which technique you use. Because Drift-fly-fishing works well there too, most Great Lakes anglers stick with one technique. However, you can be successful with floating line and a long leader while fishing every redd in a river.

For Drift-fly-fishing and any other technique, the key on redds is a very long butt section of the leader, because fly line spooks fish. Use a dull fly line—especially not the orange colored lines. Jim Johnson said, "I detest orange line because I have had it spook fish on every guide trip when the client showed up with orange fly line."

The "see through" fly lines are the best lines. The fly lines shaded green, tan or natural colors also work well. If you want a bright color try chartreuse, for some reason it does not spook fish like the orange. Whatever color of line you choose, a long butt section keeps your fly line out of a spawning fish's view.

Whether the water on the redd is shallow or deep, use the longest and thinnest butt section you can cast comfortably. The section of the leader that cuts through the surface of the water should be as thin as possible. Some anglers use as thin a butt section as 8-pound test.

Others use 10, 12, or 15-pound-test monofilament. This may be the best place in fly fishing to use a braided Kevlar type line because they are so thin compared to their strength. If you do try a Kevlar line, take special care to find

Tom Johnson with a 16-pound-plus steelhead

a knot you tie well that also works well for this type of line. Experimenting *before* you get to the river becomes a necessity—this line occasionally cuts itself when tied with most common knots.

Fly fisherman and fellow falconer, Mike Clark, uses 12-pound braid line as this *tippet* material—instead of 5 or 6-pound monofilament. He has found that its greater strength, combined with its thin diameter, creates a winning combination as he battles steelhead and salmon. The greater line strength allows him to muscle a fish away from logs and brush that would normally break the tippet. He did note that the limberness of the line created some problems with the tippet becoming knotted frequently.

While redd fishing make your tippet length (from the weight to the point fly) between six and ten feet. Its length becomes more important the more shallow the redd's water becomes. In bright sun and very shallow water, tippet should also be as long as your rod—9½ to 11

feet. At the very minimum on a shallow redd run 6 to 8-feet of tippet, to keep the weight out of the fish's view. If the weight is not visible to the fish, the steelhead will not connect its presence with the flies it encounters.

On redds the fish get the best look at the flies so the flies must act naturally. Steelhead also have a clear look at the tippet, so the tippet's diameter and color make a huge difference. On the redds, you can easily prove that you hook more fish on light tippet. Just try running 5-pound-test tippet or less. You will hook more steelhead but running a 4-pound tippet makes it tough to land fish. Anything larger than 5-pound test will mean fewer strikes.

Ultra-green monofilament is the best, but a clear monofilament would be preferable, except for its shine. Ultra-green's slight tint takes its shine out. Chameleon monofilament is often too dark for most Great Lakes conditions, which results in fewer strikes. The exceptions are rivers clouded by runoff such as the Indiana streams, some rivers in Ontario, and Upper Peninsula Michigan rivers where the high levels of tannic acid tints them.

Finding Redds

To find spawning steelhead, quietly search the river for gravel shelves covered with pea-sized stones. Steelhead select spawning gravel where a rise in the river bed increases the current speed enough to provide sufficient oxygen for egg survival. The faster current also prevents egg suffocation from silt and sand. On rivers with high banks you can walk on top of them (if it is legal), and scan the river for shadows or movement of spawning fish on the gravel. We also have someone scan the river while standing on the platform in the front of the drift boat as we journey downriver. As we drift around a likely bend or toward a historical spawning area, the guy in front scans the river from the high location. If he spots fish, we pull the boat over to a bank before the fish become alerted to our presence. Then we wade and sometimes crawl into position to cast to the fish.

On years when the water flow is low, the spawning fish will spread out over a much longer stretch of river than on a normal year. Normally the high dark water of runoff and heavy spring rains will force the steelhead upriver to look for more clear water. This pushes them into a smaller section of the river. When those conditions do not occur, the steelhead can spread out throughout the whole river system and are found spawning on whatever gravel they find. It pays to extend your search for spawning steelhead far downriver from the traditional spawning areas. The reward for your efforts will be fishing alone for unspooked steelhead—a rare treat.

Another location for spawning steelhead (and salmon) is the deep-water redds at the back of pools. The tailout of many large pools, especially those on sweeping bends in Great Lakes tributaries, contain gravel that the steelhead find favorable for spawning. These redds can be hidden from anglers by their depth. They can be as deep as eight feet or greater. We have seen anglers who "despise and detest redd fishing" unknowingly fishing a deep water redd. When we came drifting by one day, we asked how they were doing. They hollered their excitement, "We've caught five fish from the tailout of this pool!"

"That is a nice spot," I said as I kept oaring downriver.

We wondered if that is not what happens on many Western rivers as well. People who detest redd fishing accidentally and unknowingly fish for actively spawning steelhead on a deep-water redd in the tailout of a pool.

Obviously, when we wade across a river, we always look for shallow places. But during spawning season the steelhead have spawned in these locations. Therefore, never walk in a redd; if you do you will be crushing the next generation of wild steelhead. I would rather risk getting wet by wading through a deep run than accidentally stumble into a redd. If you must walk across the gravel to cross the river, be sure that you do not walk into pockets that the females have hollowed out for their eggs.

> *Because the majority of spring steelhead does not feed, cast flies that imitate what the fish see continually*

Polarized glasses are a necessity to locate steelhead and watch their reactions to your flies on all the redds locations. Early one May, I was carefully sneaking along a bank overlooking historic spawning gravel when I saw two steelhead spawning in an unusual place. They were very near my bank and behind a large rock. Small trees heavily lined the bank and only allowed two access lanes to the river. One was less than 12-feet from the fish, and the other was upriver over 30-feet from the pair. The greatest problem was that casting from there put me directly upriver from the spawning fish. That is the worst place to get a drag-free drift and to set the hook without pulling the hook out of the fish's mouth.

The casting became an effort to position the Slinky so it would pull the flies down to the shallow redd. After each cast I fed out line as the flies neared the fish. I soon became convinced that the flies were drifting somewhere near the fish, but wondered about hooking them. An upward pull of the rod would likely pull the flies out of the fish's mouth. Jock Scott offered the solution to this problem in his book, *Greased Line Fishing for Salmon (and Steelhead)*. "For instance, if a fish takes straight below you, you must drop your hand or let out slack. You will avoid the dreadful mistake of raising the rod on a strike. You must train yourself to do the opposite. Either do nothing, or drop the point of the rod toward your own bank, until it nearly touches the water. Then the pull of the stream on the line will hook the fish. But the habit is strong and the will is weak, and few times when I have done all this . . ."

> *Try fishing from your knees, standing in trenches, keeping your back away from the fish, and making longer casts*

Bill Herzog also wrote about this in the December-January '95, *Salmon-Trout-Steelheader*, "The instant a steelhead takes the bait when the gear is hanging straight below your position, instead of instinctively hauling back and 'crossing its eyes,' immediately drop the rod tip at the fish, and slowly swing the rod toward your side of the bank. This will create a few feet of slack, allowing the steelhead to turn back to its lie—the ensuing line belly forcing the hook into the corner of its mouth."

As I continued to cast to the two steelhead, I saw a steelhead open its mouth trying to dislodge something. I didn't think my flies were to the fish yet, but I set the hook anyway. *Just in case*, I thought, jerking the rod downriver and low. The fish shot out of the water and

raced downstream. I followed. Downriver around the next bend, 80 yards from the redd, I tailed a 12-pound male steelhead. It pays to use polarizing glasses and to watch the fish on each drift.

Here I had accidentally done what Scott and Herzog had mentioned. Because I could not tell that my flies were down to the fish, I was waiting what would have been too long for a normal situation. It was too long because the fish would have spit out the fly except that it got caught in its mouth and it could not dislodge it. That in turn allowed time for the Slinky to pass the fish. When I swept the rod toward my bank the hook was in the corner of his mouth. He was hooked and the fight was on.

Positioning Yourself for Redd Fishing

No one wants to depend on catching steelhead by accident like I did that day. But knowing where to stand in reference to the fish is an important factor in getting the proper drift to the fish, and catching more steelhead.

Jim Johnson said, "Position yourself just upstream and across from the fish, if you can get there without them seeing you. The ideal drift is when you start to extend the rod downriver at a 45° angle, so that the rod tip is directly across from the head of the fish. The drift will be perfect there, the line will have just drawn tight but won't be swinging yet. If fish are upriver to you, then the flies are drifting into slack, and it is difficult to detect a strike. If the fish are upriver, you will 'line' or foulhook more fish. When the fish are downriver you can make a little mend and hold the weight back for just a second. This lets the flies work out ahead of the Slinky. Then you can let the flies drift further *naturally,* by lowering the rod to feed out more line. That gives you a long, natural, drag-free drift where the fish are holding. As soon as the flies pass the fish, the weight swings the flies out of the lane and you can cast again. That way you do not waste time waiting for the flies to get into position. You spend more time with your flies in front of the fish. The cast will land almost directly across from you, if the fish are at two o'clock. But if that water is faster or deeper you have to cast further upstream to get to flies down to the strike zone."

> *The ideal drift is when you start to extend the rod downriver at a 45° angle, so that the rod tip is directly across from the head of the fish*

You must cast upstream far enough so that the Slinky touches bottom about the length of your tippet ahead of the fish. That length is the distance from your weight to the point fly. On a perfect drift the flies approach the steelhead at a 45° angle ahead of the weight. Many anglers fish so the weight goes through before the flies, but that always puts some drag or side pull on the flies.

If the fish move to the side away from the flies, put the flies six more inches apart then the fish are moving. For instance, if the fish are moving to the side three feet, put your two flies 42-inches apart. When the fish move away from one, they encounter the other fly.

Getting into position to cast to spawning fish is more difficult than most anglers think. We spook many more steelhead and salmon than we realize. Even when the fish do not leave the redd, they can be spooked. Once they sense your presence, they become much more difficult to catch. On the other hand, it does not take the fish long to forget you. If the fish become rattled, rest them for thirty minutes. Then crawl back into position before casting to them again.

Treat the steelhead (and salmon) like trophy rising Brown trout in shallow water. You will enjoy much more success than if you walk within 20-feet of them and splash your casts on their heads. If you can get into position without alerting the fish, your strike percentage is

much higher. If you alert the steelhead, your chances go down from eighty to twenty percent.

Try crouching as you approach the spawning fish, especially for the first few casts. Also try fishing from your knees, standing in trenches, keeping your back away from the fish, and making longer casts. As you do, your success improves tremendously.

Casting From Your Knees

If the river is too narrow or too brushy or if river currents are tricky, you may have to cast from your knees to catch steelhead (or salmon) effectively. Sometimes you have to cast from your knees because of the tricky currents or the lay of the fish. On the day when I first took Frank Stidham and Byron and Paul Reinhold fishing, we drifted downriver to a wide gravel flat. Here we found steelhead spawning in ten inches of water, up against a very tall and very steep bank. The fish at times seemed to disappear under the small undercut of the bank. The river was wide there, over 140-feet, so we had plenty of room to anchor the boat and prepare for fishing.

After a few casts, we realized we needed to get closer to effectively hook these fish. But if we got any closer they would see us clearly and spook. The bright day had sent nearly every steelhead looking for deep pools. So we knew that this situation was too precious to botch.

The speed of the current and their closeness to the opposite bank meant the only place to cast to these fish was from our knees while in a fast run of current. This was no small feat for these first time fly fishermen. But each gave it a try. The first one soon learned that he had to cast the flies *onto the bank*. They could then drift down to the spawning fish—a hen with two males. Each hooked a fish from that redd. Fortunately the first two each hooked a male, and the last one hooked the female. Each fish fought hard. The two males bolted off downriver once they were hooked and quickly broke the tippet. Byron was the last to hook a fish there and when the female left the redd, she bolted toward us and came right up to Byron's feet. By the time Byron got the line tight on her again, she was off downriver and free. Without casting from their knees, they would have never hooked any of those fish.

> *If fish are upriver to you, then the flies are drifting into slack, and it is difficult to detect a strike*

On another day I found fish on a redd in the middle of a 40-foot wide stretch of gravel. The water was three feet deep and the current was fast. A willow tree hung over the river and its branches were between 20 and 30 inches off the surface of the current. The willow was in the only place to cast well to these fish.

So I went downriver, crawled along the bank, then into the water, and went up under the willow branches, where the water was only 14-inches deep. That day was so warm that I had taken off my sweater and was fishing in a T-shirt—with a fly fishing insignia on it, of course. I soon realized the fish might see the flashing of my silver watch on my wrist, so I put it in the pocket of my neoprene waders.

Under the willow I sat on my heels and tried to figure out how to cast from there. The only possibility was the Drift-fly-fishing technique. I stripped the fly line and the butt section of my leader into the guides until only 3 to 6-inches of monofilament extended to the Slinky. I then brought the rod downriver and made a side arm pitch. I released the fly line with my left hand as the Slinky began pulling the line out of the guides. Here the nail knot between the butt-section of leader and the fly line became very important. The major factor that stops the cast with this method is the connection between the fly line and leader. After several failed casts I realized the dynamics of casting side arm were like throwing a curve ball—I had to aim the

cast to the right of my intended target.

Finally I began drifting the flies near the fish. Of course, my feet fell asleep. After several more casts I hooked a fish I had not seen. It was a nice Brown trout that had been dining on steelhead eggs. Then I caught a 24-inch steelhead that was laying back off the redd because the larger males would not let him come any closer. I landed both of those fish without moving from under the willow tree. Finally I hooked a steelhead I had been targeting. That one brought me to my feet and I tailed her downriver. When I released her she did not immediately go back to spawning, so the redd became vacant. That one sequence of casting from my knees saved a whole day's fishing. The bright day had pushed almost every steelhead into the deep pools except the ones by the fateful willow tree.

How Far From The Fish?

When you think about how far to stand from the fish, do not think about distance from the fish—although 30-feet might be a minimum—think about angle.

In very shallow water keep low so the refraction of the water distorts your silhouette. In shallow water the fish are closer to the surface, which makes it easier for them to see you. If you get fish in three or four feet of water, you can get fairly close to them. If they are in one to two feet of water, you are in trouble, especially if the surface is glassy. It always pays to keep brush behind you. Keep your silhouette broken and wear drab clothing—avoid bright colors.

Jim Johnson said, "I have spent some fruitless days trying to guide anglers who insisted on wearing orange hats and jackets. Fish see the intensity of that color. Too often, I have been standing watching a redd full of fish and have had an angler with an orange hat and jacket sneak up alongside me to see the fish, and the whole school spooked. That has happened lots of times."

Successful Redd Flies

Because the majority of spring steelhead does not feed, cast flies that imitate what the fish see continually. Use the flies they accept as natural to that redd, like Caddis, Stoneflies, and egg patterns. Mayfly nymphs also work well if they are natural to that river and season. Another effective fly is the egg-sucking type pattern, such as egg-sucking leeches, minnows and nymphs. These flies take advantage of the protective reflexes of the spawning fish. The two best flies for actively spawning steelhead are the common naturals or the egg-sucking patterns. Small flies work better than the bigger ones. However if the water is dirty or the sky is very overcast, use up to Number 6 flies, but none bigger on the redds.

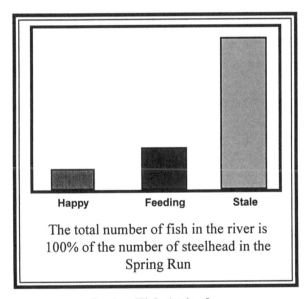

The total number of fish in the river is 100% of the number of steelhead in the Spring Run

Spring Fish Attitudes

Some fishermen have success on big Number 2 or 4 egg-sucking leeches in certain conditions. But the larger your fly, the greater chance it will intimidate spawning steelhead rather than stimulate the protective reaction. If the flies look too unnatural they will spook the fish, but the natural looking flies have a much greater success rate. Stay within the natural food item's size range—between ¼ inch to 1½ inches long.

Jim Johnson said that he usually has an egg-sucking Leech at the point fly and a Caddis as the dropper fly. These flies allow you to see where the Leech fly passes through the redd, then you can adjust the Leech so the fish will move *toward* the Caddis. You simply run the Leech, which you can see, to pass just outside the fish and the Leech fly moves the fish in to confront the Caddis. As the Leech passes on the outside of the fish, the Slinky hits the bottom and darts the Leech toward the fish. The steelhead then moves to the inside, where the Caddis is waiting for him. That is how to use the bigger fly to move the fish to the small fly.

When you run two small flies or two natural flies, then both flies work fish back and forth to each other. Usually the spawning fish move around to some degree on the redd. With the small flies, which you cannot see in the water, you must cast repeatedly until the above sequence happens accidentally. The movement of the fish on the redd is yet another reason for fishing with two flies. If you misjudge where the fish are or make a poor cast, one fly may still hit the fish's strike zone. That alone will increase your success.

One of Jim Johnson's favorite egg-sucking patterns is an egg-sucking Sparrow fly—a Sparrow nymph with a plastic bead ahead of it. Tom Johnson's favorite fly is his cream P.M. Wiggler with an orange bead. To some anglers Tom's P.M. Wiggler may appear as a scrimp pattern, but there's no scrimp in the P.M.

If the water is high and cloudy, fish a black or brown Marabou Wiggler (a Woolly Bugger with squirrel tail pulled over its back) to attract strikes. The murky water makes the smaller nymphs less visible, and fortunately it makes the steelhead feel well protected and thus less timid. The Neon Wiggler—I must admit—catches fish under these conditions too. A Neon Wiggler is tied like a Spring's Wiggler with a Chartreuse chenille body, neon red hackle, and a neon red Egg Yarn for the tail and wing. The yarn wing replaces the squirrel tail wing of

Spring's version. You may also tie this pattern by reversing which parts you make neon red and chartreuse. One day while we were fishing dark murky water, we found a redd under an overhanging tree, which was just upstream of a famous pool on that river. The males were attacking each other so frequently, we could not get a single drift to them before they moved to chase another fish.

Finally, after almost an hour of casting every other fly, I reluctantly—my old fishing prejudices die hard—tied on a Neon Wiggler. On the second cast a male steelhead charged over and bit it. It was easy to set the hook because he had done it already for me.

Yet another very effective pattern is the Glow-in-the-Dark Nymph. Because it glows in the dark it works well in murky water, and in other low light conditions such as early morning and dusk. It is tied with cream-colored glow-in-the-dark latex Squid legs—

see it better, the Glow-Nymph proves effective for poor visibility conditions. Oddly enough, I used it for spawning steelhead in six foot deep, gin clear water, on a very bright day. When steelhead rejected other flies, they took the Glow-Nymph with relish. I do not know why, but it worked.

Hare's Ear Nymphs are as productive at imitating insects and attracting strikes from steelhead as they are from trout. I always carry Hare's Ears nymphs in sizes 6 through 12. The Green Caddis Larvae pattern (in sizes 8 and 10) will catch bright steelhead in pools, especially those downriver of spawning redds. Odd-

Mack Filkins (age twelve) with a Steelhead

from the Squid that salmon and steelhead trollers use. The nymph is tied with a cream marabou tail, a glow body and thorax, a wing casing of turkey wing, and a brown hen neck for hackle.

The Glow-Nymph is tied on a Number 6 Spoat hook, or another hook with a medium length shaft. Because salmon and steelhead can

ly enough, most of the 12-pound-plus steelhead I have caught were hooked on a Number 10 Green Caddis, tied around the bend of a short-shanked Number 8 hook.

Number 10 Caddis Larva flies are simple and quick to tie and they also catch 20-pound-plus pound Chinook salmon, but that's the next chapter. . .

The Sport of Kings . . . on Flies

Fly Fishing for the Great Lakes' Largest Migratory Salmon

Fall is an outdoorsman's season of opportunity. Huge King Salmon migrate and spawn in the rivers. Bucks create scraps and rubs near bow stands. Flocks of turkeys cackle, dance and fly through the colorful autumn forest. Spaniels flush grouse and pheasant from the brush. Squirrels dig through golden leaves for their hoard of winter treasure. And my trained Harris' Hawk yearns for flights at feathered and furred quarry.

Fall *is* the season of opportunity—too much opportunity. It's a love/hate relationship, really. I love all the outdoor adventures that it offers and hate my inability to enjoy all of them continually.

With so many outdoor opportunities to enjoy, I reflect on why I always chisel some days from September and October to fly fish for King Salmon as they migrate up the rivers.

Why? Well, the answer is a story.

A King's Day

On September 21, two of my closest friends, Al Renner, Tom Jared, and I went Chinook fishing on our favorite Lake Michigan tributary. The Kings in the rivers that fall were huge and numerous. That Thursday was very dark; the layer of thick clouds created a heavy overcast and very humid morning. Tom oared his driftboat downriver to the first bend from the landing while Al and I quickly switched from our dark polarized glasses with amber lenses. With the cloudy darkness it seemed near sunset all day long. At the river's first bend we found a pod of salmon in the pool.

We wondered aloud about fishing so close to the landing, with several miles of great river ahead. Tom oared the boat over to a shallow sand bar and we rigged up for a session with these Kings. Tom and Al tied on Osprey™ shootingheads, but I had decided to experiment with several techniques and tippet lengths that day. I began with the Drift-fly-fishing method and 18-foot leader and tippet rig.

This pool allowed only one of us to fish at a time. Al fished first, he had caught many salmon before but not on a fly gear. Tom and I watched and chatted as Al fished. Talking was as much a part of the day as fishing because the year before I had moved two hundred miles north to Sault Ste. Marie. We greatly anticipated this day for the friendship as well as the fish. Waiting for a turn to fish posed no problem.

Al fished for fifteen to twenty minutes before he broke off his flies on a submerged log in the pool. The salmon moved around constantly in the pool as they fought each other. Occasionally, we got a glimpse of one huge King that dwarfed the others. Obviously, he ruled the pool, but the other salmon were persistent. After he broke off, Al said, "One of you guys give this a try while I retie. I apparently can't catch one of these salmon. They won't strike."

> *The two best flies for actively spawning steelhead are the common naturals or the egg-sucking patterns*

"Maybe you should tie on a longer tippet this time, Al," I suggested as I motioned for Tom to wade into position for casting. "The longer tippet, like seven or eight feet, will get your flies twice as far away from Osprey™, and you'll get more strikes."

"I don't think that the shorter tippet is spooking these fish in the pool," Tom commented as he cast his Osprey™ shootinghead with the same length tippet as Al's. "These fish aren't moving from the pool. They're moving because of the attacks of that huge Chinook. That's him *right there!*" Tom cheered pointing into the pool.

By that time, I was standing in the bow of

Tom's drift boat where I could see the silhouettes of the salmon in the pool. "Wow, that's a huge one!" I said.

> *It always pays to keep brush behind you. Keep your silhouette broken and wear drab clothing; avoid bright colors*

Tom cast into the pools for several minutes without a strike, when the line stopped abruptly on one drift and he set the hook quickly. The rod bent double and we cheered, but there was no throbbing on the end of his line.

"It's just a log," Tom moaned. "Likely the same one Al hit." Moments later, Tom had broken off his point fly, "Kenn, you try this time."

"Just tie on a point fly, and keep fishing," I said from my perch atop the boat. "That huge salmon just came back into view."

Tom retied quickly with his Clinch Knot tyer and began casting again. A few minutes and many casts later Tom snagged up again on the same log. This time he lost all his leader.

"You're up, Kenn," Tom said, wading back toward the boat.

This time I slipped down into the river without protest and picked up my rod. It was rigged with an orange and yellow 2-Egg cluster fly as the dropper fly and an imitation Sparrow nymph—which I had dubbed the 'arrow-nymph. Above the 'arrow-nymph I had slid on an orange smooth translucent plastic bead, which made it into an egg-sucking nymph.

At the time, I knew my first two casts were not into the strike zone of the salmon. I was casting to keep away from the log my friends had hooked. On the third cast, however, the line paused in the current and I struck. Instantly a thrashing salmon rose to the surface of the pool. We all cheered!

"Did you guys hear that *crack* when I set the hook?" I asked.

"I did," both said in unison.

"That was my rod," I said. "I've heard that noise before."

Fortunately, the salmon stayed in the pool to fight the other salmon. None of us could clearly see which of the salmon I had hooked. As I tried to pressure the fish more, it bulled away from me, toward the cluster of logs in the far bend of the pool. The salmon responded to the pressure and returned to the pod of fish. A few minutes later it charged again toward the logs and I pressured it again. This time the rod snapped in two a couple feet above the cork.

"Isn't that your 10-foot, 10-weight Tarpon Rod?" Al asked.

tape. The fight resumed, but as I held the cork handle with my left hand and squeezed the taped section with my right, I felt tremendously disadvantaged. I was. Less than two minutes later the fish broke the tippet. The rest of the day I fished with a spare rod that Tom carried in his driftboat. Fortunately, the broken rod had a lifetime guarantee that was honored by St. Croix.

We went through the rotation again at the first pool and soon it was my turn again. This time I used an 8-weight rod and the same rigging and flies as before. Within a few minutes

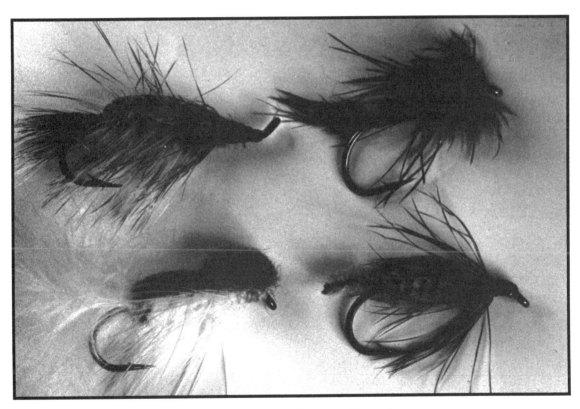

Spring Wiggler Sparrow Nymph
Neon Wiggler   'arrow Nymph

"I'm afraid so," I replied. "Tom, do you have any duct tape in your boat?"

"No," Tom said chuckling. "But I have a First Aid kit."

Tom got out a roll of white medical tape. We overlapped the two sections of rod about eight inches and he quickly wrapped it with

I had another strike. The fight began the same but this time the rod did not break. The salmon tired after about 15 minutes of fighting the other salmon before he realized that I was fighting him. Finally, I could pressure him from the pool out onto the shallow gravel bar downriver. He bulled his way back into the pool three times before I turned him away from the pool for good. Tom manned the net and four minutes later, a bright male Chinook salmon was in my grip. The King measured 41-inches long, had a girth of 22-inches and weighed 27-pounds. Black spots dotted his olive colored back. The olive tone melted into a flesh-tone color on his stomach. His jaw had not metamorphosed at all. He looked like a fish caught trolling on a Great Lake except olive replaced his silver color. He had been hooked in the tongue by the 'arrow-Nymph with the orange bead in front of it.

We had no camera.

> *When you think about how far to stand from the fish, do not think about distance, think about angle*

I walked back to the closest fly shop and bought a waterproof disposable camera. We took a few pictures, but it was too dark for quality photos with that type of camera. Because of the beauty of this fish, I planned to mount it. I pulled a nylon stringer from my fly vest and tied the fish to the side of the boat. There it would keep fresh and alive so we could take more pictures if later the clouds dissipated enough to provide light.

We fished the same pool until 1:00 P.M. and all three of us hooked and fought fish from it. Tom even hooked and fought that "king of the pool" but did not land it. We all fished with longer tippets and with the Egg Cluster flies and 'arrow-Nymphs with orange bead.

Once we left that pool, we headed downriver and every few minutes I glanced over the side of the boat to make sure that the King was as huge as we thought he was. After we rounded the second bend, I glanced again at the salmon and . . . He was gone.

The metal ring on the end of the stringer had broken at the weld and my salmon had disappeared. I learned a costly lesson about purchasing expensive rods and reels, then buying a 98¢ stringer.

That day, we each fair-hooked at least 12 to 20 Chinook salmon but only landed four. As Jim Teeney had told me that spring, there is a time each day when the fish "go on the bite." That afternoon, when Tom oared us past other anglers, we soon realized that they *all* had fish on. It still was very dark from clouds. We soon stopped below a set of riffles where the river spread out to over 150 feet wide. There we fished a stretch of river 200 yards long. Tom fished just below the riffles. Al fished a pod of spawning Kings on a huge gravel bar. I fished below Al, at another set of redds along some logs near the far bank. We all hooked and landed fish there. Every few minutes, two of us would hear the other yell and look up to see him fighting a salmon. It seemed that someone had a fish on all the time. Then we began targeting just the huge fish we found.

Three different times, two of us had salmon on at the same time. Once, all three of us were fighting Kings simultaneously. Tom landed his. Al's fish brought him quickly down to where I fought my fish. Just when I thought we might all land these fish, Al's fish was off. He had intentionally broke it off when it came near my fish. Al thought it would make me lose my fish. After I cursed Al for breaking off his fish, he proceeded to tail my salmon.

Now back to the original question. Why do we chisel time of out a hectic fall schedule to chase Chinook?

Huge fish. Warm days. Tough fights. Bright leaves. Broken tippets. Great friends. And the "big one" that got away, even after it has been landed.

That fall I went on a quest to catch *another* King salmon that was 41-inches long so that I could mount it. No easy feat.

Kings of the Fall Migration

King salmon, also called Chinook salmon, are the largest of the Pacific salmon that have been introduced into the Great Lakes system. These salmon leave their spawning rivers and pasture in the Great Lakes until they reach their sexual maturity, at three or four years of age. Then in fall they migrate upriver to spawn and then die. These fish generally range from 15 to 30-pounds but some salmon weigh in at 35-pounds and larger. You quickly realize these salmon can be brutal on light tackle.

late September and October. However some Kings actively spawn through November and into early December. Coho salmon, where they are present, also migrate into the rivers in these fall months, but their timing is a few weeks later than the Kings.

Joe Cain, the Director of the Sault Ste. Marie, Ontario Sport Fishing Development, said that all the Coho in Ontario tributaries are self reproducing and self supporting. They are all migrants from plantings by Michigan and other states, because Ontario has never plant-

Joe Cloud and Byron Reinhold—Successful Chinook Fly Fishermen

Some Chinook enter the rivers as early as late August, most migrate in September and October. Many females will begin spawning in September, with peak spawning period in

ed Coho. Joe Cain reported, "Even without any stocking there are some nice tributaries in northern Ontario with good (sometimes great) runs of Coho salmon."

How To FIND Salmon . . .

Chinook salmon strike flies when they gather in pods in the deeper water around the spawning redds. Flies solicit strikes from salmon that pause in holding pools on their upstream journey; like the areas where we find fall and spring steelhead as they migrate upriver.

King salmon seek the same things as steelhead when migrating upriver. Locate them in the same ways as you would summer steelhead. Try the steelhead techniques and locations that we mentioned earlier. Salmon often use the same spots on the river—pools, runs, and redds—as steelhead. The main difference is that the salmon spawn on gravel that steelhead would never use. Kings use much more marginal locations and they use larger gravel than the steelhead.

> *The King measured 41-inches long, had a girth of 22-inches, and weighed 27- pounds*

Unlike steelhead and Atlantic salmon, all the Pacific salmon—Kings, Coho, and Pinks—do not leave the river after they spawn. They stay upriver until they die.

Spawning King Salmon in Your Neighborhood?

I wonder how much great salmon fishing is missed each fall because we journey to the popular rivers and ignore the Great Lakes tributaries near our homes. Your neighborhood rivers may hold a surprise for you, as one did for me. One river near my home has a stretch that most anglers and canoeists ignore in October. It has spawning salmon.

The Kings in this stretch are mostly unmolested by anglers and smack (even large, gaudy) flies with reckless abandon—much like I imagine Alaska salmon striking. Because they have not been fished, hooked or spooked, these salmon provide great (and willing) sport. They are also hard to land. So much more the fun.

On many tributaries of the Great Lakes, the spawning gravel salmon use depends upon the river conditions that fall. When the water flow is low the spawning fish spread out over a greater length of the river, and they spawn on whatever gravel they can find. On years when the river flows high and dark the salmon tend to move up more quickly, searching for clear water. On those years the fish become concentrated into a shorter stretch of river. This means that you may find salmon in one area one year and not the next, but the fish can still be in the river in the same numbers. You may have to search for them a little harder, but they are worth the effort.

Stealth and King Salmon

King salmon are famous for becoming aware of fishermen and still staying on the spawning redd. Not that all King salmon will stay but a surprising number of Chinook—as compared to steelhead—will continue to spawn even when they see fishermen nearby. This may give the angler the false impression that the salmon do not care that he is there. This is far from the case. As we discussed with spawning steelhead, salmon become harder to catch once they are aware of your presence. Stalking King salmon like you would steelhead or Brown trout will increase your success proportionately. The more stealth you use, the greater chance you will catch salmon.

Another exciting aspect of fall salmon fishing is catching Kings at night. This is true "fishing blind." George Deutscher and I have fished in no light conditions with great success. We were most successful on a stretch of river that we knew intimately—we did not want to go swimming. Also you have to know the river well enough to know where the salmon are likely to be when they come out at night to spawn.

John Kilmer, a friend and professional fly tyer, also reported great success while night fishing for Chinook. John said that especially late in the season, when most of the salmon are battle worn, he still caught many fresh salmon that were out only after dark. Nighttime is the best time to target heavily fished rivers because the shy, fresh salmon feel secure in the darkness when all the rest of the anglers have gone home. You have the river all to yourself.

The flies that John, George and I found most successful for these late night sorties were large streamers and glo-nymphs. The large streamers include any of several traditional streamers. Black was the hottest night color and flies up to Number 4 and 2 worked very well. Some tinsel also helped. George and I had great success with Woolly Buggers and Glow-Nymphs sizes 4 and 6.

At night, always fish a stretch of river that you know well and one that is easy to wade. Also, take along a partner and a flashlight. Flashlights with a flexible neck that attach to your vest pocket work best. The flashlight becomes essential when landing fish, finding your way back to the truck, and putting the glow in your Glow-Nymphs. Cast and fish without light, then once you get a fish on, turn on the light to beach, net or tail the King.

> *Huge fish. Warm days. Tough fights.*
> *Bright leaves. Broken tippets.*
> *Great friends.*

John and I both think that we foul-hooked fewer salmon in the dark. Maybe this is because we cannot target fish as closely because obviously we cannot see the fish. Therefore to get a hookup the salmon must strike the fly.

Salmon Techniques

All three types of fly fishing techniques work on King salmon in the same ways and times that we described for steelhead. In early fall when you are searching for salmon in the pools downriver of the spawning gravel, traditional techniques work especially well. Swing large streamers through the pools to these fresh,

happy salmon and you will soon find where they are holding. Use lead-eye streamers if you are so inclined. Also try the 5-inch Bunny fly we spoke of with the steelhead. Other especially successful flies include streamers with beads, blades and worm bullet-weights added. These gaudy flies attract strikes from Kings from a greater distance than traditional flies, especially from pods of fresh salmon. Traditional techniques also work when fishing shallow salmon redds, but use an extra long tippet.

> *Position yourself just upstream and across from the fish, if you can get there without them seeing you*

Horsing Kings with an Osprey™

Osprey™ shootingheads work best for searching for Kings in early fall in the pools and runs. They also work well on shallow redds and shallow pools if you keep the tippets long—at least seven to eight feet.

One fall Tom Jared and I fished with condensed shootingheads for salmon for the first time. I left Tom fishing for a pod of Kings that swam aggressively in a deep run in front of a redd. I waded downriver around a bend to check out another stretch of river. As I returned, I saw Tom with his rod bent double. Since it was too far to yell, I put my index finger in my mouth and jerked like setting the hook—a way to ask if the salmon was hooked in the mouth.

Tom nodded, "Yes," so I began to run against the current to help him land the salmon, which was now charging downriver with Tom in tow. Moments later Tom came into shouting distance.

"Swing him this way and I'll tail him," I said as I slipped on a knit glove and watched the fly line slice through the water toward me.

When he swam into view, I looked up at Tom, "That's a huge salmon," I yelled.

"I know, Kenn, I've been fighting it," Tom replied matter-of-factly.

Paul Reinhold with a King Salmon

"I'd better get the net," I said as I headed upstream to the driftboat.

After ten more minutes of fighting and two miraculous retrieves—one from an undercut bank and another from heavy brush—the hooked jawed King salmon was netted. He now hangs on the wall in the Farwell Trading Post. I thought I had caught a nice King that day until we put it next to Tom's fish. Then it looked like a "Horse and Pony Show." Tom had the horse and I had the pony.

Drift-Fly-Fishing for Kings

The Drift-fly-fishing method works the best of any fly fishing technique. Its success rate is unsurpassed for fair-hooking fish in any situation. Its success is directly proportionate to its ability to put the flies in a drag-free drift and

down to the eye level of the salmon. I very pointedly tried each technique on fall King salmon and the results were the same as those we discussed with steelhead. Small wonder that Drift-fly-fishing is the most popular technique for Great Lakes steelhead and salmon.

Gearing Up For Kings

Gearing up for Chinook salmon means assembling gear specifically for heavy fish. Most rods under 8-weight put you at a real disadvantage. Rods up to 10-weight are not too large, if you can stand casting the beast all day. An 8-weight rod that is nine feet, or preferably longer, with a stiff butt section, will greatly aid in the landing of Chinook monsters. Most of the disk-drag reels used for steelhead will serve you well for Kings. However, some lighter disk-drag reels do not apply heavy enough pressure to stop even an average sized Chinook.

Having said all that, I once caught a 22-pound-plus hen Chinook while fishing for Pink salmon. I was fishing with my Pink salmon gear—a 4/5-weight, 7½-foot trout rod and an Orvis single action reel with 4-weight fly line. When all the Pink salmon disappeared from the run at once and a pair of Kings swam into view, I began casting to them, without thinking of the consequences. A couple minutes later, one struck a brown Woolly Bugger. The current downriver was torrid and I knew I could not follow her. So I just stood there with my rod high and watched with joy, convinced she would swim off and break my 5-pound tippet.

She swam downriver in front of a huge boulder then promptly swam across the current and up onto a gravel bar where my brother, Leroy, was fishing. The hen salmon then proceeded to swim between Leroy's legs and *stop*. Leroy was looking down between his feet at the big fish, then he looked curiously toward me, eighty feet upriver.

"Well, grab her, Leroy!" I yelled.

He bent down and grabbed her with both hands around the tail. And she was landed.

An amazingly lucky feat, as if I have to tell you that. I would hate to depend on that type of coincidence to land a King salmon every time. Better to gear up properly and give yourself a fighting chance. After all, very few of you have a *handy* brother named Leroy.

Tippets for a King

Like steelhead, King salmon are selective about tippet sizes. The problem is that Chinooks come in sizes up to XXXXL. Though you can regularly land steelhead on 5-pound-test line, when King salmon get into the high twenties and low thirties, they become difficult to handle on 8-pound-test monofilament. Here is where the new Kevlar type braided lines may have the most advantage for fly fishing. You get a higher line strength with a smaller diameter. The problem will then become more broken rods.

One day my youngest son, Drew, and I fished for a pod of Chinook with a borrowed rod from my father-in-law. His pride and joy rod was a 13-foot noodle rod

blank built into a fly rod. It cast a fly as smooth as silk. On that day the salmon had continually beat us up hard. We had hooked several fish but were yet to land any on 6 and 8-pound-test line. Finally, we changed to 10-pound test tippet—not knowing this was two pounds heavier than the rod's design. A few minutes after changing to the heavier tippet I hooked a particularly large male King. The fight went on for over sixteen minutes and I had turned him three times. But I failed to realize that he had not yet seen us. Finally, I brought him close and he saw Drew with the net and bolted toward the logs in a nearby pool. I pressured him with the strength of the reel—which did not have a smooth drag—and then we heard a loud crack. It sounded like a small caliber rifle shot. The rod was broken. Try

Drew Filkins (age ten) with a King Salmon

to explain that one to your father-in-law.

That was a tough lesson to learn about using too heavy a tippet for the rod. We generally use 8-pound test tippet, but occasionally when the fish are reluctant we switch to 6 or even as low as 5-pound test. John Hunter told me that he will even use as small as 4-pound test for Chinook, but how can he land a King on 4-pound-test line? At times, I use 10, and even 12-pound test tippet if the Kings will still strike the flies. I have learned to set the drag on the reel to what the rod can handle, and to never—well, almost never—add pressure to the reel with my hand.

Chinook Flies

Flies Fit for a King

Selecting flies for salmon is not as simple as tying a gob of silver tinsel on a 2/0-hook and chucking it into a pool. Successful salmon flies come in three basic types: egg patterns, attractors/streamers and naturals.

> *King salmon are famous for becoming aware of fishermen and still staying on the spawning redd*

Egg patterns are popular flies for Chinook with good reason. They work. The simplest egg pattern is just clipped Glo-Bug® yarn attached to a hook. A more complex but very successful egg pattern is the Egg Cluster pattern. Good colors for egg patterns include chartreuse, yellow, pink, orange and combinations of the colors. If I had to pick just one egg pattern to take on the river, I would take a 2-Egg Cluster fly in orange and yellow.

John Hunter refuses to use an Egg Cluster fly for King salmon on redds until the female is the only fish left. John said, "If we use an Egg Cluster fly the female will often take it. If we use other flies such as streamers and nymphs, we can catch the males that are fighting for the female. If we use the Egg Cluster we will catch her before the males. She gets the first crack at the fly because she is positioned ahead of the males. If we catch her then that spoils the redd. The males have nothing to keep them there so they move off the redd. That makes them harder to find."

The second category of flies is attractor/streamer patterns. They include bright streamer patterns, Egg-Sucking Leeches, Muddler Minnows, Woolly Buggers, Spring Wigglers, Neon Wigglers and (adaptations of) Atlantic Salmon patterns. Streamer flies can be as simple as wrapping silver tinsel on a hook and putting a red, olive, or purple bucktail wing on it. Bright colors like chartreuse, yellow, neon red, and bright pink also catch salmon. Green Butt Skunk is another excellent pattern for Chinook—especially at night. Woolly Buggers tied in black, brown or olive are very effective.

One night while I tied flies for our next day's salmon excursion, my eleven-year-old son, Drew, sat beside me to tie flies. He tied some normal salmon patterns, then he tied a streamer with a white marabou tail, a white body wrapped with silver tinsel, and some white hackle for the neck. I tried to sound hopeful that his new creation would work, but I did not hold much promise for it. My fishing intuition failed me again, because the next afternoon, soon after Drew tied on his white salmon streamer, he hooked and landed his first salmon on a fly. Oddly enough, about ten days later John Hunter gave me a fly that was much like Drew's creation in color, size and silhouette.

The third category of flies for every salmon trip is the naturals. There are days on the river when salmon will refuse most egg patterns and attractor flies. On those days you will want some nymph flies tied on strong hooks—strong enough for 20-pound-plus fish. One October day, we cast our normal assortment of successful salmon flies but got few strikes. We lightened our tippets, but still no success. When we came upon John Hunter, he suggested we try nymphs, especially green Caddis Larva on a Number 10 hook.

> *All three types of fly fishing techniques work on King salmon in the same ways and times described for steelhead*

I was skeptical, but desperate. We tied on a Hare's Ear nymph and a Green Caddis fly, then hooked and landed a salmon on the second cast. Then we realized the amount of green Caddis activity in the river that day. We continued to hook fish the rest of the afternoon. On other days when the fishing was slow, we hooked several salmon on Hare's Ear nymphs, Hex-nymphs and Stonefly nymphs. Always include Glow-nymphs in your fly box for night fishing and even for very bright days in shallow water.

A fake Sparrow nymph, an "'arrow-nymph," is an olive wet fly with a grizzly hen heck hackle wrapped at the collar. It can be fished alone or with an orange plastic bead in front of it to emulate a salmon egg—this makes the fly an "egg-sucking nymph" pattern. This is a deadly fly when the fish on the redd refuse all other offerings.

If I could only take one fly from each of the three categories for a day's fishing I would take an orange and yellow 2-Egg Cluster, an olive Woolly Bugger, and an olive 'arrow-nymph.

The Quest . . .

I went on a quest after I lost that mountable 41-inch male Chinook salmon. In the end of September and early October I became so focused on catching a huge salmon, I would not cast in to a pod of salmon unless I thought it contained a fish over 40-inches. That fall I caught three more salmon 41-inches long. Two were caught within seven minutes of each other. I caught most on an egg-sucking 'arrow-Nymph tied on a Number 6 sproat hook.

The first one came after several days of not landing any huge salmon. On one of those days, I hooked a fish that I estimate was over 30-pounds on 8-pound test tippet. I hooked him four times that day and never even came close to landing him. The following day, I hooked him again from the same redd, fought him for over twenty-four minutes before I lost him. Why? We will see that in Chapter 10, *fighting and landing huge fish.* Like my friend said, "Everyone is good for something, even if it's just to be a bad example!"

"... Yes, this is the Preacher,
... Can I call you right back, I'm on the other line?"

Pink Salmon—*Honestly* Unbelievable

As a clergyman I know Ministers are not supposed to lie. But I did.

It's no excuse, but I thought everyone would *think* I was a liar if I told the whole truth.

I told people that in odd calendar years, we saw schools of four hundred Pink salmon. That was not the whole truth. I said "four hundred Pinks" because I thought no one would believe that we really saw schools of *one thousand* Pink salmon in the Midwest.

Now *that* sounds like a lie doesn't it? Just another fisherman's exaggeration. But it's not.

Really.

Pink salmon fishing is honestly unbelievable.

I took one photo of 144 Pink salmon in a 10-by-20 foot section of a river. The Pinks were that thick over an entire 40-by-40 foot area.

Really?

Okay. A 60-by-60 foot section of river!

Fishing during the fall run of Pink salmon during the odd calendar years offers Alaskan-type fishing without the remoteness, the grizzly bears, or the long trek across the continent.

Pink salmon enter the rivers during the last week of August and build to unbelievable numbers in the pools and runs that they use as staging areas before spawning. It's not uncommon to see Pink salmon as well as Chinook salmon porpoising from the pools as they aggravate each other. In this aggravated state they strike flies with devastating consistency.

Pink salmon are Pacific salmon that range in size from two to four pounds with some fish in the five pound class. Pink salmon also go by the name Humpback salmon. The males go through a spawning metamorphosis to obtain a hooked jaw and a humped back that gives them their nickname.

Pink salmon mature in two years so the strongest and largest runs of Pink salmon have been in the odd calendar years, though the even year runs are becoming stronger all the time. Pink salmon are aggressive spawners and the males belligerently defend their territories, which makes them particularly vulnerable to anglers.

Bright, female Pinks fight like rainbow trout or small steelhead. These females are the most acrobatic fish in the river, at times they even seem to dance across the surface. The male Pink salmon wage a different kind of battle. They usually bull their way deep into a pool, or turn their broad side to the current and pressure you with the added strength of the river.

What Pinks lack in size, they make up for in aggression, numbers and availability. The Pink salmon's sheer numbers and aggressive behavior is a prescription for angling excitement.

A Brother's Revenge

That is what my brother, Leroy, and our friend John Silvas found out—even during an "off year" Pink salmon run.

John and I have fished steelhead and salmon for some time but Leroy had just begun to fish with us. Leroy had heard our fishing stories and decided to come along. Thus far steelhead had proven to be Leroy's nemesis. He had hooked several on flies but had not landed one.

When Leroy hooked his first steelhead on a fly, it jumped and darted downriver as the reel screamed its protest. I wondered how that steelhead could get forty yards downriver so quickly while pulling against the drag.

When I turned to tighten the drag on Leroy's reel, I said, "Ah, Leroy, you're reeling the wrong way." By then the steelhead was so far downriver that it broke him off easily. He blames me—and my legendary poor netting skills—for losing his latest battle with a bright male steelhead. Fortunately that's a story for another time.

All that added a significance to this day, Leroy's first encounter with Pink salmon. With his luck catching cold-water migrants, I commemorated the event by tying a special fly for the occasion.

The night before we went, I tied Egg Cluster flies, Woolly Buggers, Perch Streamers and several other successful patterns, when the idea for the new fly pattern for Leroy came to mind.

Sitting at the vise, I decided, "If Leroy is going to catch a Pink salmon, he needs all the help he can get. So I'll take *all* the bright tying materials that catch salmon and put them on one fly."

It turned out to be a streamer fly with Neon

144 Pink Salmon in one school

Red chenille for the body, and a Chartreuse chenille wrapped over it creating a Barber Pole effect. The wing of Leroy's fly began with bright green Flashabou tinsel, and was covered with two wings of Krystal Flash tinsel, one Neon Orange and one Neon Pink—for pink salmon of course.

> *An eight foot, 4 or 5-weight fly rod with a single action reel is sufficient to handle Pink salmon*

The result was a perfectly ugly, absolutely gaudy streamer that looked like a rodeo clown who had dyed and frizzed his hair. I was confident that this fly would *not* catch a fish and would positively repel them.

Now it needed a name. Bright as a rodeo clown, it was dubbed "Leroy's Lasso."

I tied two. One for Leroy to use, another for posterity—and for the tales back home. I had the story mostly written. "Leroy's Lasso vs. the Pink salmon. Final score: Pinks 45—Lasso 0."

That was the perfect fly for my brother's first attempt at Pink salmon—one problem though—I forgot to tell the salmon.

On our drive to Michigan's Upper Peninsula I described the fly, its invention and finally its name. Leroy took the ribbing in good fun; he even planned to fish with his fly. Maybe he would have thought differently had I told him the fly's projected success rate. But God has His way of dealing with reprobate Preachers—especially those who fish.

That September morning we waded into an upper Michigan tributary of Lake Huron and saw Pink salmon schooled behind a large rock in the middle of the current. Once we got to the other side, John fished at the head of a large pool.

"Try a Woolly Bugger and an Egg Cluster first," I suggested. "That tandem has been very productive. The yellow and red Egg Cluster fly attracted over half the strikes last year."

Leroy prepared to fish the Pinks we saw holding in a run below a series of redds. It was shallow enough to see the fish grouped together when the sun peaked between the clouds that dumped rain on us most of the day.

"Pink salmon are spawning upriver at that riffle," I said to Leroy as we stared into the run looking for any moving shadows.

"The salmon hold in this fast run as a staging area before they spawn. I usually dead-drift the flies through this run, then feed out line and sweep them through the tail-out. Below this tail-out the current drops into that dark, deep pool where John is fishing. That pool holds Pinks, steelhead, Chinook salmon and resident river Rainbow trout."

I smirked as I tied on a Leroy's Lasso and an Egg Cluster fly to the 6-pound tippet of Leroy's fly line. I tied the egg fly as the upper fly and Leroy's Lasso as the terminal fly, 36-inches apart.

> *The Drift-fly-fishing method works the best of any fly fishing technique. Its success rate is unsurpassed for fair-hooking fish in any situation*

"The floating eggs suspended from the hook by thread undulate in the current like natural salmon eggs." I told Leroy as he examined the Egg Cluster fly. "The eggs and thread get caught in the salmon's teeth and allow you more time to set the hook."

Leroy nodded to me, then cast upriver and drifted the flies down through the salmon. Holding his rod high, he kept as much of his fly line out of the current as possible. He watched the fly line for any pause in the drift as the current pushed the flies through the fast run. No strike.

Several casts later, as the flies approached the Pinks, a huge torpedo-shaped figure swam upstream through the pocket and all the Pink salmon scattered.

"What is that?" Leroy asked pointing the rod at the dark shadow.

"A Chinook salmon from that pool," I said. "The Pinks give those monsters a wide berth. They'll return in a couple minutes."

And they did. A few casts later the line paused, and Leroy set the hook. The line drew taut and the rod tip quivered from the shaking salmon.

"You got him!" I cheered.

Leroy already knew it.

The salmon turned its broad side against the current and bulled away from him. Then yielding to the pressure, it turned and darted downriver. Leroy waded down with it and moments later, his first Pink salmon was in the net.

Leroy's Lasso

"Which fly did he take?" John asked.

"Leroy's Lasso," I replied.

Leroy smiled, "So, my fly might really work."

"Maybe. . ." I said as I turned to John and shrugged.

Half an hour later, John and I were still fishless. Leroy had landed two more Humpback salmon. Both males. Both on Leroy's Lasso.

"Hey Kenn, do you have another Leroy's Lasso for me to use?" John asked as I netted Leroy's fourth salmon.

"Sorry John," I said. "I only tied two and Leroy doesn't seem to want to share."

Leroy smiled.

Minutes after we went back to fishing, Leroy hollered again, "Fish on!"

As I grabbed the net a Pink salmon sur-

faced, then another salmon rose just behind the first. "Look at that!" I yelled. "These salmon are so aggressive that a second male is attacking the one on the fly."

When they surfaced again, it became clear that Leroy had *both* salmon on his line. "Hey John, Leroy has two Pinks on—one on each fly!"

As John scrambled up the bank to see them, Leroy fought the salmon. Once, they surfaced close enough that I saw a fly in each salmon's mouth. It was unbelievable.

But true.

Pink salmon had taught me to trust the unbelievable.

As Leroy fought to land the salmon, the tippet scraped over some jagged rocks and broke. The Pinks were free. One Leroy's Lasso was gone.

Leroy moaned.

"Well John, at least he didn't land them," I said. "We would have *never* heard the end of that."

"Has either of you ever had two salmon or steelhead on simultaneously?" Leroy asked.

We shook our heads.

"Has either of you fished with the Leroy's Lasso?"

We shook our heads again.

"Leroy's Lasso strikes again!" he cheered as his smile widened.

That smile was nothing like the one he had two hours later when he hooked another double of Pink salmon. That day Leroy and John landed over 30 Pink salmon and lost many more. That would be considered a poor day of fishing on a strong year run of Pink salmon.

Rivers Flowing Pink

Pink salmon entered the Great Lakes fishing equation either by accident, an act of God or through lack of foresight. One story of their introduction claims a helicopter transporting the yearling Pinks for planting in Canada encountered foul weather over Lake Superior and dumped the fish to escape the storm. A second story claims that a Canadian hatchery built on a tributary of Lake Superior flooded and the salmon were swept into the lake.

Leroy Filkins and Norm Anderson with Pinks

One Canadian fisheries authority told me that in 1956, yearling Pink salmon in the Dorian Hatchery in Thunder Bay, Ontario were slated for release in the Albany river system, which drains into the Huron Bay. The Ministry transferred most of the salmon and released them there. The rest of the Pink salmon somehow got released into Dorian Creek, which runs through the town of Thunder Bay. The Pink salmon became successful in Lake Superior and in the following decades spread down through the St. Mary's River (the natural spillway for Lake Superior) into Lake Huron and Lake Michigan.

However, G.W. Ozburn, the Chairman and Professor of Lakehead University in Thunder Bay, Ontario wrote, "Pink salmon were certainly never a planned introduction for Lake Superior. . . Apparently success with this program [the Albany River project] was at the best marginal and the last remaining fish were dumped out with the hatchery discharge water into the mouth of the Current River in Port Arthur (now amalgamated with Fort William to form the City of Thunder Bay). This hatchery had been operational at the mouth of the Current River for many years although it has since been closed."

The Dorian hatchery, which is still operational, had no connection with the Pink salmon release.

However they got released into Lake Superior, the Pink salmon have spread rapidly throughout Lake Superior then through the St. Mary's River into the upper Lake Huron and Lake Michigan. Ironically, Pink salmon are almost nonexistent in their target waterway, the Albany River system.

Fishing writer Jim Bedford wrote, "Pink salmon have a short life cycle of two years. Their short river stay probably helped them adapt and flourish in the big freshwater seas. With their two-year life cycle, populations of Pink salmon in the West usually only run every other year. Since the only release of these fish occurred in 1955, you would expect migrations only in the odd numbered years.

"However, probably due to the cold water of Lake Superior, some salmon have taken three years to mature and make their spawning run. This we now have runs every year but there continues to be a tendency to have larger influxes of fish during the odd numbered falls.

"In the ocean, Pink salmon feed almost entirely on plankton. So you would wonder why there should be any concern about these diminutive salmon eating too many smelt and alewives. Well, repeated analyses of stomach contents showed that it was obvious that the Humpies in the Great Lakes do eat small fish. Probably the plankton densities were not high enough so they adapted and added small fish to their diet.

"Could it be that this new fish diet and an extra year in the lake was just what was needed to produce monster humpies?"

Big Catches and World Records . . . Oops!?!

While releasing any fish over their limit, two informed anglers can catch fifty Pink salmon a day.

"Could that be true?" you ask.

Okay, the whole truth . . . They can catch over 70 Pink salmon in a day. I told you that you'd think me a liar. I'm now coming clean.

In 1992, Great Lakes Pink salmon caused quite a stir with reports of an all tackle world record Pink salmon, caught on the St. Mary's River.

"The Michigan State record for Pink salmon was broken twice in 1992. The second fish will likely be accepted as the 'all tackle world record,' while weighing in at 14.05-pounds. B.L. Jacob of Iron River caught the 31.2-inch Pink salmon on August 23, 1992 while trolling a northern king lure in Michigan's DeTour Passage. Jacob, a retired Michigan Department of Natural Resources fisheries biologist, broke the Michigan record set just ten days before by David Comba of Sault Ste. Marie, Ontario,

who trolled the same area with a northport nailer on August 13, 1992. It weighed 11.73-pounds and broke the old record set by the 8.56-pounder from the Carp River caught by Ron Karasek in August, 1987."

Upon further investigation the fishery biologist realized these huge Pink salmon were in reality a natural hybrid between Pink salmon and Chinook salmon. They were then dubbed "Pi-nook salmon."

> *Some salmon have taken three years to mature and make their spawning run, so we now have runs every year. But there continues to be larger influxes of fish during the odd numbered falls*

I have seen a few Pi-nooks caught on flies, and caught two one September. The Pi-nooks I saw did not weigh over five pounds, but I am still looking. It is easy for me to account for this natural hybrid between Chinooks and Pinks. Within casting distance, I have very frequently seen a pod of 50 to 100 actively spawning Pinks. Suddenly they all scatter as a pair of Chinook salmon swim onto the redd. The Kings then begin to spawn and soon the female King starts dropping her eggs and the male Chinook then fertilizes them with his milt. The hen had just laid her eggs where the Pinks were spawning. As the male King deposits his milt, he fertilizes many Pink salmon eggs along with the Chinook eggs. This sequence happens repeatedly during the fall spawning season. The result is a natural hybrid Pi-nook salmon. My next quest will be to catch a large Pi-nook to hang between my Chinook and Pink salmon mounts.

A Boy Turned Pink

Late one March while we were cross-country skiing with the Pahn family of our Church, their nine-year-old son, Brian, spoke of his love for fishing. He mentioned making rubber Creepy

Crawlers to fish with, but said "they didn't catch any fish." I told Brian, "They certainly will catch fish and next September I'll take you after Pink salmon."

All spring and summer Brian made Creepy Crawlers in anticipation of *the trip*. Finally after school one rainy Tuesday, I picked up Brian and his older brother Will and we went to the river. Brian put on my knee-high rubber boots over his shoes and I threw him over my shoulder like a sack of potatoes. I then walked out to a gravel bar in the middle of the river and placed Brian on a rock. I rigged Brian's rod with a Drift-fishing system and two bare hooks upon which I put one fluorescent orange and one fluorescent green Creepy Crawler.

The pod of Pinks in front of Brian looked like a thick black blob. After a few minutes, Brian got the casting motion down, and he began to catch Pinks. He caught so many Pinks—about one every third cast. Honest. I was so busy landing Brian's fish that I could not get Will's rod rigged. Finally, I told Brian to fight his next fish until I got Will ready to fish with regular flies.

Both began catching Pinks. They landed over 35 fish in the couple hours before dark. About halfway through that time Brian caught the nicest and largest Pink I had seen all season. He caught it on a small orange Creepy Crawler. We had released all the other fish but I thought this one would be good for photos if the weather cleared. A little while

later I began tying flies on Brian's tippet because the Creepy Crawlers kept coming off the hooks. Some time later, Will caught a nice female Pink salmon so we took both fish home to show their parents. When they weighed the fish, Brian's male weighed 4-pounds and Will's hen was over 2-pounds.

Brian fish was a Michigan Master Angler class fish. The next afternoon, Brian's mother took the male to be officially weighed. The fish was automatically entered in the Sault Ste.

Brian Pahn with his "Master Angler" Pink Salmon

Marie Salmon Derby. When it was over, Brian won first place for Pink Salmon. At the awards banquet Brian got a plaque and a rod and reel—but not a fly rod and reel. Brian told everyone that he caught the trophy Pink salmon on a Creepy Crawler.

Now no fisherman at that banquet will ever look at a Creepy Crawler quite the same way again.

Pink Migration

Pink salmon begin migrating to the mouths of the tributaries and up the rivers in mid-August each year. The greatest concentrations of Pink salmon are in Lake Superior with many Pinks in the upper regions of both Lake Huron and Lake Michigan. The St. Mary's waterway in northern Lake Huron is so full of Pink salmon that Joe Cain, the Director of the Sault Ste. Marie, Ontario, Sport Fishing Development Center, told me the local charter captains become annoyed with the Pink salmon striking the lures that they intend for Chinook salmon.

Almost all of the tributaries of Lake Superior—including streams in Michigan, Ontario and Minnesota—have runs of Pink salmon.

> *The right technique and willing fish are no replacement for experience. Luck also plays less a part of fishing than most realize*

If you have a favorite stream in Minnesota, upper Wisconsin, Ontario, Michigan's Upper Peninsula or in the northern tip of lower Michigan, give it a try this fall. Pink salmon seem to expand their spawning range every year. In 1991, I saw a male Pink salmon caught at Bawanna's Bend on the Pere Marquette River—that's halfway down the east coast of Lake Michigan! Also, they have been caught on Indiana's small streams. Pink salmon can migrate far, but don't go there expecting to find them in great numbers.

Spotting Pinks

In the rivers, look for Pink salmon on the gravel bars where you would find spawning steelhead and Chinook salmon. Pink salmon often look like dark shadows in the river bed. Stare at the shadows for few minutes looking for salmon to move from the group or swing their tails. If after some time you're still unsure about the shadows, put your flies through them a couple times. Pink salmon seem less selective about redds than either the steelhead or Chinook, so look in even marginal spawning areas.

> *While releasing any fish over their limit, two informed anglers can catch seventy Pink salmon a day*

There is, however, one time when the Pinks *are* very reluctant to strike. It is when they school for their journey upriver. For instance, when Pinks are migrating in schools and they reach a dam they begin to swarm around looking for passage upriver. Then very few Pinks will strike a fly or any other lure or bait. They stay in this reluctant state until they settle into a pool, run or redd, then they again take flies with surprising regularity.

The only real success I have had with these schooling passage Pinks was with Greg Steere. We tried every trick we knew before we got a few strikes by putting a tiny Colorado spinner blade and a tiny orange (or chartreuse) bead ahead of a Number 10 black nymph. It makes no sense to me, but only that would get strikes.

Pink Gear and Technique

An eight foot, 4 or 5-weight fly rod with a single action reel is sufficient to handle Pink salmon. The light fly rod provides for a fun fight. But if you plan to fish for Chinook salmon on your trip, take along your 8-weight rod and a disk-drag reel.

Of all the fish we have mentioned, Pink salmon are the most amenable to any of the fly fishing techniques. Especially when they are on shallow redds and defending their territory. The Western steelhead techniques and flies will work especially well because these happy Pink salmon mimic many traits of the Western steelhead. Two-handed salmon rods also work well,

Pink salmon eggs with an egg cluster fly

also Spey flies and Atlantic salmon patterns and techniques. Osprey™ type shootingheads work well and Osprey™ were actually designed through their success on Pink salmon.

Drift-fly-fishing works especially well for deep or fast runs (or deep *and* fast runs) and deep pools. Drift-fly-fishing is the best technique for these locations because while the others lose their effectiveness, Drift-fly-fishing keeps its success rate high.

The right technique and willing fish are no replacement for experience. Luck also plays less a part of fishing than most realize. One day Byron Reinhold and I fished for Pinks in the same run—Bryon fished the head of the run and I fished the middle. We were less than 40-feet apart. Byron was in the best spot, but I constantly caught more fish. Bryon was almost fishless. When he gave me an odd look after I landed yet another salmon, I asked Byron if he wanted to switch places. He did. But when we switched I started catching *a lot* more fish this time, because it was the best spot. Soon we switched back. The result was the same. We switched rods and used same flies, same Slinkies, same tippet, but we got different results. The difference? Experience. Especially on this run. I had fished it for six years. I also had trouble fishing it the first time or two. That night his wife asked Byron, "How did it go?"

"Well, Nancy," Byron said, "I now say for sure that fishing is not just luck. It is a skill."

My favorite technique for Pinks combines a dead-drift nymphing with a streamer swing added. First, I take a position slightly upstream and across from the target pod of fish. Salmon, as far downstream as can be reached with the rod tip, are in the dead-drift target zone. With an eight foot fly rod the salmon should be within 11 feet downriver—the eight foot rod plus a three foot arm.

> *Pink salmon have taught me to trust the unbelievable*

To fish the dead-drift area, cast upriver so the flies drift directly into the salmon's nose. The distance you cast upriver of the holding fish depends on the depth and speed of the current. Pink salmon can hold in runs as shallow as one foot. Strike indicators can help, but watching visible salmon is more effective. After the flies pass through the drag-free zone, target the fish holding behind them. Feed line and sweep the flies into the tail-out of the pool or run. Be alert, because strikes often occur on the sweeps, especially on streamers and Woolly Buggers.

Pink Flies or Flies for Pinks?

Whatever fishing technique you use for Pink salmon, don't get too stuck on the hot pink color that looks like someone spilled Pepto-Bismol in your fly box.

When I first pursued Pink salmon everyone told me to use hot pink lures. On that trip for Pinks I went armed with neon pink Woolly Buggers, hot pink yarn egg flies, pink nymphs, streamers tied with neon pink Krystal Flash and pink Bunny Leeches. Admittedly, I caught a few Pink salmon on these flies but pink was *never* the most effective color on any day. If I had to pick just one color for all my Pink salmon flies, I'd pick olive. Well, maybe yellow. Or black.

When Pink salmon first settle in to a pool or run, they take streamers and nymphs constantly. A "Perch Streamer"—a bucktail streamer with a green wing and gold body—works well. So does the same pattern tied with a fox squirrel-tail (or marabou or bear hair) wing. Brown, green or black Woolly Buggers tied with long webby saddle hackle are also effective—especially if tied with some sliver Flashabou. *Hexagenia* nymph patterns and Caddis Larva patterns are also productive.

> *Look for Pink salmon on the gravel bars where you would find spawning steelhead and Chinook salmon*

Once the salmon begin to spawn in earnest, bright flies lure most of the strikes. The salmon in the staging areas take the eggs drifting from the hundreds of spawning Pink salmon on the redds upriver from them. The single most effective pattern that I've found is the Egg Cluster fly with its floating eggs.

Around half the salmon we catch during an "On-Year" run are caught on Egg Cluster flies, though the salmon always have a choice between the Egg Cluster and its tandem fly, like a streamer or a nymph.

Other bright flies that attract strikes include Glo-Bugs® yarn patterns in chartreuse, yellow, orange and pink. The best color is chartreuse with a splash of orange tied into it. Woolly Buggers tied in chartreuse, yellow, white, and red also attract strikes from Pink salmon. Any bright fly with lots of color also attracts strikes. Leroy's Lasso did very well; much to its creator's dismay, Chinook salmon greatly enjoyed that fly. If steelhead like it, and Leroy keeps fishing, Leroy's Lasso will be my nemesis.

> *When Pink salmon first settle in to a pool or run, they take streamers and nymphs constantly*

When fishing a pool, run or redd, try one color, then when the fishing slows, try the same pod of fish with that fly in a different color. You will catch more fish from the same pod. Don't forget to bring some Creepy Crawlers!

When you are fishing Pinks on a redd, there are often so many fish that you cannot keep from foul-hooking some of them. When there are a hundred fish on a redd in front of you, it can be tough to run your flies through at nose level without hooking one, especially the tall humps of the males.

You can land Pink salmon easily enough without a landing net by grabbing them by the tail. Though with the news about the huge Pinook salmon caught in Great Lakes tributaries, I'll be carrying a net every time this fall. Honest.

Fighting Big Fish On Small Rivers

Part of the allure of fly fishing for steelhead and salmon is fighting large and sometimes huge fish. The challenge is knowing that some fish you will never land, and others are only landed because of sheer luck. Take that Chinook I landed on a 4/5-weight rod, for example. Our goal is to increase our success percentage by practicing strategies that increase our landing rate. I know I would have landed more fish if only I had been thinking about what I was doing. But sometimes you just respond by reflex. . .

For example, take the first trip that Al Renner and Rick Higgins experienced together in my driftboat to fly fish for steelhead. I was fishing a deep-water redd just upriver of a fast slot between two log jams that choked the river. By coincidence, Al was standing behind me when I hooked a nice male steelhead that turned and charged downriver. As he went down-

stream, he swam into the logs near our bank and continued down. I followed him downriver by wading through the fast deep slot.

As I entered the slot I slipped on the gravel and went down up to my shoulders. When I regained my balance I realized what the steelhead had done. By reflex I reacted; I had never thought of this action before, much less planned it. Watching the line pass under the submerged log, I imagined the line guiding the rod tip through the brush. In part because I was already wet, I submerged the rod in the water and the fly line guided the rod through the logs. With my left arm submerged to my shoulder, I reached on the other side of the log and grabbed the rod with my right hand.

When I lifted the rod the line pulled tight and the fish surfaced 30 yards downriver on a shallow gravel shelf. Al and I waded downriver to get the fish back within the 45° area. The fish kept fishing itself down current and was about to enter a brushy pool. Because Al is allergic to fish, I handed him the rod and went to tail the steelhead. As I waded toward the fish he opened his mouth, shook his head and dislodged the fly. I turned to Al and shrugged.

"I cannot believe that you stuck that rod through these logs," Al exclaimed. "I'm not man enough for this fly fishing stuff!"

"Apparently, neither am I!" I replied.

That is part of the lure of chasing these migrants with fly tackle. There are some fish that

Fish spawning on a redd

cannot be landed. The fish above was a landable fish. But some fish you cannot land with anything short of a 6-0 treble hook, cable, and a "pool cue" with guides.

We could make a long list of the fish that got hooked and just swam off without looking back. Jim Johnson told me that the steelhead will go wherever it wants on its first run. If it does not get into the brush on the first rush, you have a chance to land it. Once you have a fish on for 30 seconds you have a much higher chance to land it. But that first rush can be devastating.

Often we have had steelhead tear off upriver after they were hooked and they just keep going until they break the tippet. I remember this specifically happening twice while fishing the dark water of early spring run-off. In each case, I was fishing on speculation because water visibility was so low. When I set the hook, the fish, which I never saw, simply tore off upriver until the tippet broke. Their power is impressive. Chinook have often done the same. Dan Graham hooked a King salmon out of a run and it took off upriver. About 150-feet away it jumped and snapped the tippet. Some fish will not be landed.

Landing Rules

There are five habits that once developed will increase your landing successes:

❈ Set the hook with a "low and down river" sweep of the rod to drive the hook into the fish's jaw

❈ Fight the fish in an area no more than 45° up or down river from you

❈ Tire the fish with the rod low and to the side

❈ Create a fighting/wading plan before you cast to the fish

❈ Land the fish by beaching, tailing or netting it.

Setting the Hook

The first step in landing a fish is making a solid connection with the fish—solid enough to endure the strain of the fight. Set the hook

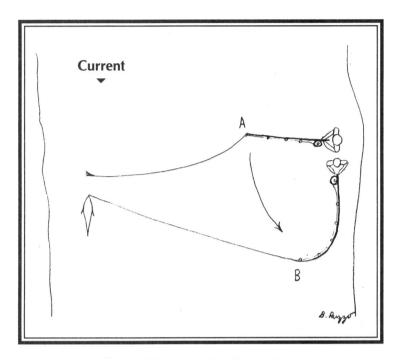

View of hook setting from above

by swinging the rod low to the water and downriver. Keeping the rod low and downriver takes the belly out of the line more quickly. If you set the hook "upriver" or raise it straight up, you are pulling the fly line against and through the current before you apply any pressure to the fish. When you swing the rod downriver and low the current works as your assistant in setting the hook.

If, as we discussed, you keep your target fish between twelve o'clock and two hours downriver, then when you sweep the rod downriver the rod tip should be almost directly across the current

from the head of the fish. Then the force of the hook set will drive the hook into the jaw of the fish. If you set the hook upriver, you are pulling the hook toward the front of (and out of) the fish's mouth.

Another aspect that is tough to teach first-time steelheaders is to set the hook with some force. Drive the hook into their jaw. Do not make a halfhearted hook set. When the flies are drifting through the strike zone, hold the extra fly line under the fingers of your right hand. Then set the hook grip down tightly and jerk the rod back hard. Once the fish is on, get all the fly line onto the reel as quickly as possible. I cast and fight fish with the rod in my strongest hand—I'm right-handed. I set my reels to crank with my left hand. Many anglers cast with the right hand and then switch to the left hand to fight the fish and crank the reel with their right hand. To me this never made any sense. Fight-

Proper Hook Setting:
Sweep the rod down current and low to the water

ing these fish is tough enough without giving them one more advantage.

Once the fish is hooked, it is important to keep the line tight to the fish. When my oldest son, Mack, caught his first Chinook salmon on a fly he was eleven years old. On that bright October day, he was fishing a pod of fish in a dark run near some salmon redds. Once he hooked the King it jumped three times and darted off downriver. Fortunately it was a long series of redds where he could wade and fight the fish. As Mack fought the salmon, nearby anglers cheered, "Keep the line tight!"

I waded downriver trying to get into position to net his fish, when the salmon leaped out of the water again and simultaneously I heard a huge splash. When I turned back to see Mack, he was gone. All I could see was his rod sticking out of the water. Then he popped up like a cork, with his rod in hand. He had tripped on a large submerged rock and for an instant the fish was in the air and Mack was under water. Yet even while immersed, he kept the line taut. A few minutes later, a drenched boy held his first Chinook salmon.

The exception to the rule of keeping the line tight occurs when the fish runs downriver and you have no recourse to stop it. Then you must point your rod downriver and let the fish run until it decides to stop. Your only prayer is that it stops in a pool and does not get wrapped up in some brush or logs. As the fish goes

downriver, follow it and take up any slack line as you wade downriver. When you get to the pool where the fish stopped you will soon realize if you still have a fighting chance. The percentages of landing a fish after such a run are not great. But they are higher than the percentages you would have otherwise—ZERO. When a fish gets downriver more than 45°, the

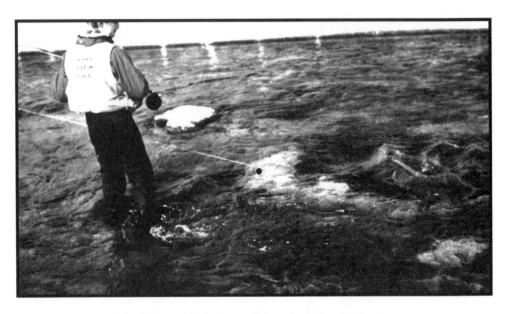

John Kilmer fighting a fish using the 45° Rule

advantage is in the fish's favor. Keeping the fish within that 45° zone is no easy task, but it is easier than the alternative.

The 45-Degree Rule

The best place to control a fish that you are fighting is between 45° upriver or downriver from where you are standing. As you stand looking across current that is 0°, locating a point 45° upriver and downriver will create your best fighting zone. The goal in the fight is to put *side* pressure on the fish, tire it, and turn it from obstacles. When a fish gets out of your 45° zone, you have little control over its direction and are applying little pressure to tire the fish.

To keep the fish in that 45° zone, you have to move with it as it swims down or upriver. Generally, the fish will turn downriver in a fight, especially as it tires. A friend once lost "the largest steelhead I had ever seen," because he refused to move when the fish went downriver. He intended to fight the fish from the spot where he had hooked it. He did fight it from there, but soon lost the fish.

John Silvas once fought a Chinook salmon that took him downriver two hundred yards to a pool in the bend of the river. I knew from experience the pool was not very deep, but the water clarity was very poor that day. As John and I watched the fish pull out line toward the pool, I realized the pool was not deep enough to let the salmon pull out that much fly line. So I waded out into the pool and found John's line around a log. After I slipped if off, I held it taut as I walked back to John and he reeled in the excess line. When I got back to John, the leader had appeared from the current and he found that the Chinook was less than seven feet from him! After all that, we lost the fish anyway.

Obviously, when you select a location to fish from, keep in mind you must fight the fish that you hook. You put yourself at a real disadvantage if you fish from a bank where trees keep you from moving during the fight or where the water is too deep to wade. Ask Tom Fetters about the situation we found him in one day while steelhead fishing. Fetters was fighting a fish when we came downriver looking for him. Because he could not fight the fish from the bank, Tom Jared waded out from the opposite bank to get the rod from Fetters. The water was deep and Fetters could not reach out far enough to hand Jared the rod. So I waded out to help Jared get closer, but we both began slipping on the gravel and we each got wet. Finally Fetters jumped into the pool and swam with the rod until he got his footing. By then we were all wet and the steelhead had entangled Fetter's fly line in several logs. As we waded out of our "swimming hole," a couple of driftboats came past, we must of looked like a live rendition of *"Larry, Moe, & Curley Gone Fly Fishing!"*

Fatiguing the Fish

Once the fish has been solidly hooked, and you wade to keep it within the 45° rule, the next key is to tire the fish. You accomplish this by fighting the fish with the rod low and to the side. You want to fatigue the muscles in the fish's sides. If you hold the rod high, you put *vertical* pressure on the fish, which essentially rests the fish. Fish negotiate their vertical position in the water by inflating and deflating their air sacks. This does not require much muscle fatigue at all. When you put vertical pressure on a fish, all it does is deflate their air sacks, and you put virtually no stress on the fish. This may be why anglers have had very long battles with fish in deep pools. It is tough to tire a fish under those conditions with light tackle.

> *If you put side pressure on a fish you can fatigue its side muscles very quickly*

If, however, you put side pressure on a fish you can fatigue their side muscles very quickly. To apply side-pressure on the fish, keep the fish within the 45° zone and keep your rod tip close to the river. While fighting remember that the 45° zone is determined by the relationship of the fish to your *rod tip*. For instance, if the fish is only nine feet away and is straight out from you in the current, he is directly *downriver* from your rod tip. He is out of the 45° zone of the pressure of your rod. In that case simply swing your rod high—to keep the line tight—and over to the downriver side. This puts the fish back into the 45° zone from the rod tip and puts pressure on its muscles. If the fish then comes too close to your bank, walk out into the current and swing your rod toward the far bank. Then pull the fish away from your bank.

Sometimes when you hook a fish, it is so intent on spawning or fighting it ignores that it has been hooked. In such cases, simply apply pressure to the fish. Do not worry about pulling the fish from the redd or away from the pod, let the fish weary itself by fighting the other fish and you. The more fatigued the fish becomes, the easier it is to fight and land it. The fresh 27-pound Chinook salmon I mentioned earlier was landed on 8-pound tippet because he wearied before he knew he was fighting me.

A smooth disk-drag reel is a very important tool for applying pressure while fighting fish. Before you cast to a pod of fish, set your reel tension for the size of your tippet. Set the reel tension to around 1½ to 2-pounds for 6-pound-test tippet. Remember, the rod multiplies the tension

Fighting and fatiguing a fish

created by the reel, and the soft tip section of the fly rod protects your tippet. I am convinced that I have frequently set my reel tension too high and lost fish because they broke the tippet. Once I lightened the tension on my reel, I landed more fish. You can test your tension through your rod and reel by tying a gallon plastic milk jug to your fly line and filling it partially with water. Just remember "*a pint is a pound the world around.*" A quart of water is two pounds. A half gallon is four pounds. A gallon of water is eight pounds. Put in enough water to test the strength of your tippet and knots. When you find the right tension for the tippet weight, trust it. Keep your hand off the reel.

My college friend Tom McNerney had never landed a steelhead until the day we fished together. Tom fished one redd for over four

hours, and hooked over 12 steelhead. First Tom landed a five pound male, then an eight pound male. Then he hooked a huge steelhead, which I think was 20-pounds. Tom fought it downriver 120 yards until it paused in the fast current just outside some huge boulders. I stood in an eddy inside the boulders. Then the steelhead rolled onto its side, only six feet away from me. I was sure we would land it, we were only 30 yards from a huge slow pool—a perfect place to land this monster.

"He's on his side," I cheered turning back to Tom. "We'll land him down at . . ."

I did not get the last sentence out, when I saw Tom's hand reaching for the reel. Tom quickly grabbed the reel handle to put greater pressure on the fish. He then backed up to pull the steelhead into the eddy. As I turned back toward the fish, it rolled upright, turned out into the fast current, and easily snapped the 6-pound tippet.

I did not realize the size of that male until a half hour later, when Tom landed a female steelhead. He asked me how much the hen weighed, I guessed it to be seven or eight pounds. It looked so small compared to the male he had just fought. But when we weighed the hen it was almost 12-pounds. Then we reconsidered how huge the male must have been. We could have known, if he would have kept his hand off the reel.

> *An often overlooked aspect of salmon and steelhead fighting is planning a wading and fighting strategy*

Oddly enough there are times when you do *not* want to stress and pressure a fish. You can keep from stressing a fish by holding your rod high. This keeps the line tight and allows the fish to calm down and possibly stay still for a moment. This is a useful technique in situations such as when your fly line becomes a "bird's nest"—a tangled series of knots and loops. Then lift your rod and rest the fish while you cut out the bird's nest.

To remove a bird's nest during a fight, hold the fly line under your rod hand, then strip the line off the reel so the nest hangs free. Have your fishing partner (this procedure is difficult to do solo) cut the fly line both above and below the knots. After he reties the two ends together, crank the knot up onto your reel. If you are lucky the fish will not pull that knot through your guides. The success rate for this procedure is not great, but what are your choices? It is worth a try. I have twice tried this method and we lost both fish. However, I have seen others do it successfully.

A better solution is to keep the bird's nest from happening at all. Generally they happen when the fly line is wound on to the reel without proper tension. Run your fly line through

your rod hand when you reel it in. If the fly line is reeled in loosely, when a fish puts great stress on it, it tangles up on itself. An event best avoided.

A Wading/Fighting Plan

An often overlooked aspect of salmon and steelhead fighting is planning a wading and fighting strategy. A predicated wading/fighting plan greatly aids the landing of fish during a fight. The plan considers where you will wade and what obstacles you must fight the fish away from. Generally, a hooked fish will turn downriver during a fight, so plan your basic strategy in that direction. As we mentioned earlier, Tom Fetters had no plan when he hooked a steelhead at a deep bend in the river. A plan helps.

> *The best place to control a fish you are fighting is between 45° upriver or downriver from where you're standing*

On another day, Tom Fetters hooked a steelhead that turned downriver. We knew that if it got into the deep run on our side of the river, it would be lost to the logs. So Tom had to cross the river and wade along a brushy bank, where the only footing was a two-foot-wide clay ledge. I brought the net and waded with Tom as he fought the fish. At the ledge I grabbed his jacket and we walked the slippery clay ledge together. Once I slipped and held myself up by holding Tom. Seconds after I regained my footing, Tom slipped and my stability held him from a cold swim. Soon we waded onto a large sand bar and Tom easily landed the steelhead from there. Without that wading plan, the fish would have determined our fighting course. He would have been lost to that first deep run, where we had lost other fish.

Some fishing stretches become so familiar that you fight fish at them by reflex. I have fought so many fish down a stretch of St. Mary's Rapids that I know which foot will hit which rock as I scamper down to a deep pool. Also, I have had practice wading out into the fast current halfway down the run to slip the fly line around a Toyota-sized boulder. Still, that does not mean that I land all the fish I hook there. It does mean that I have a fighting chance.

Best Laid Plans . . .

Even the best laid plans do not mean that you will land every fish. One September day, Al Renner hooked a male Chinook on a redd above a stretch of river that my sons call "Ping Pong Alley." Ping Pong Alley was created by a terrific flood on the river that moved a huge log jam to the middle of a narrow, fast run between two quick curves in the river. They call it "Ping Pong Alley" because our driftboat bounces like a ping pong ball when we drift through that run. We always hit the logs with both sides of the boat. I think it is their way of commenting on my oaring skills—or lack thereof. Though Ping Pong Alley is tough to navigate with a driftboat, it is an even harder place to land a fish.

After Renner hooked the Chinook, it instantly tore

downriver, around the bend toward Ping Pong Alley. Al was in tow, and when the King got to the large log pile in the middle of the river it went through the shallow outside run. Three long, thin cedar trees were laying in the water. The Chinook went under one of them and kept going. When Al got to the cedar he glanced back at me and said, "He went under that log— here I go."

With that Al submerged his rod and stuck it under the log. He got it under and pulled out the other side but the fly line was still snagging a branch of the cedar. Before Al could get

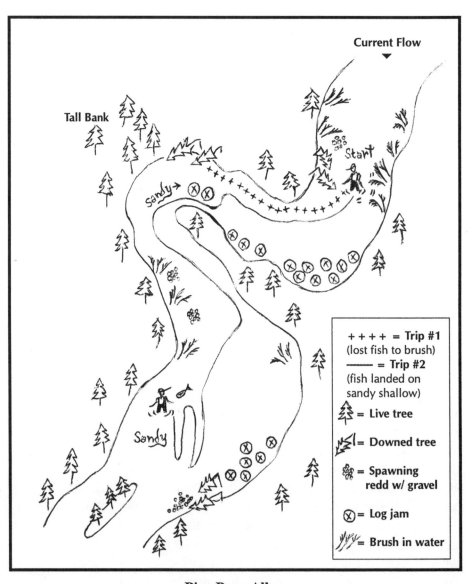

Ping Pong Alley

it off, the Chinook broke the tippet. Al shook his head. I pushed the cedars back along the river bank so he could fight the next fish without the trees.

Later Al hooked a hen from that same redd, but she stayed at the redd for several minutes while Al fought her. Finally she fatigued enough to turn downriver and soon Al was with her at Ping Pong Alley. Instead of following the shallow run that we had cleared, she went through the deep fast run on the far side of the log jam. Al looked at me and asked, "What do we do now?"

"We follow her," I shrugged. "There's nothing else to do. We may get wet," I concluded. I grabbed the back of his jacket for support as we waded through the run.

"Follow this edge then turn right at that log," I coached. "Trust me Al, I've waded here several times. This is the only way to keep from swimming. Now, let's wade along the log pile then walk around behind them."

Surprisingly, we made it through without filling our waders, and the fight continued down a long, fast, waist-deep run before she swam into a huge corner pool. From that pool Al fought her for at least twelve more minutes. Several times he brought her to the edge of the pool, but she simply bullied her way back into the deep water. Finally, she wearied enough for Al to pull her into the knee-deep water on a sand bar. There a friendly angler netted her with a huge salmon net. That hen was Al's first salmon on a fly. She was a bright olive, 39-inch long fish with a girth of 21-inches.

John Hunter tailing a steelhead

Beaching, Tailing, or Netting

Once the fish wearies and you decide to land it, you have three choices: beaching, tailing, and netting the fish. Beaching is a good option if you fish alone and if the river has a place to beach it. A sand bar is the best place to beach a fish. Once the fish becomes fatigued, keep the leader as short as possible and walk up onto the sand bar. When the fish has difficulty moving because of the shallow water, grab it by the tail.

If you cannot find a place to beach a weary fish then tail it. It is an exciting way to land a fish alone. Wear a knit glove on your tailing hand so your fingers do not slide off the fish. Make sure to wet your hand before you grab the tail, this helps protect the "fish slime" on the fish. The slime is the fish's protective coat-

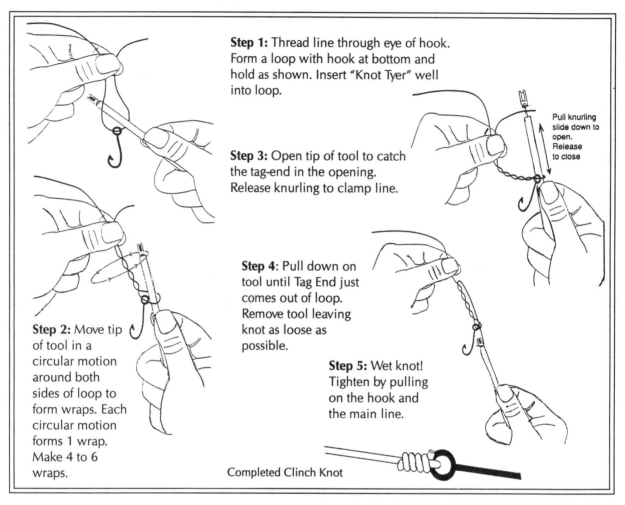

Step 1: Thread line through eye of hook. Form a loop with hook at bottom and hold as shown. Insert "Knot Tyer" well into loop.

Step 3: Open tip of tool to catch the tag-end in the opening. Release knurling to clamp line.

Pull knurling slide down to open. Release to close

Step 2: Move tip of tool in a circular motion around both sides of loop to form wraps. Each circular motion forms 1 wrap. Make 4 to 6 wraps.

Step 4: Pull down on tool until Tag End just comes out of loop. Remove tool leaving knot as loose as possible.

Step 5: Wet knot! Tighten by pulling on the hook and the main line.

Completed Clinch Knot

Clinch Knot

ing, which you do not want to disturb when you plan to release the fish. Some huge fish are hard to tail because of the size of their tail. A useful tool for tailing huge fish is an Atlantic salmon tailer—a wooden handle with a cord on one end to loop around the fish's tail.

Netting a large fish is not as easy as you may assume. Some anglers believe in the head first method, while other think that it should be tail first. When netting a fish, the netter should get downriver of the fish and the fisherman lets the fish drift back into the net. My experience as the Nimble Netter has shown that black hooped nets spook fish less than the bright silver ones. Also be careful about netting a fish that is hooked on the point fly. The dropper fly can become caught on the net (when

the fish is not netted). When the fish makes its next run it will quickly break the tippet. Believe me—this has happened!

Knot Tyers & Tippets *(see page 134)*
One very useful tool for landing steelhead and salmon is a knot tyer. My favorite model is the brass Clinch Knot Tyer. A fly fisherman can sometimes tie literally hundreds of knots in one day on the river. With spawning fish in sight, I get in a hurry when retying flies. No one generates more poor knots than a rushed angler. With the Knot Tyer, however, you can tie better knots consistently and quickly. With some practice, rigging with a Knot Tyer is at least two or three times faster than hand-tying the knots. My favorite knot is the Double Clinch

Step 1: Lay end of Leader in groove of tip.

Step 2: Insert end of Fly Line into the groove starting at the tip and passing under all the wraps.

END OF FLY LINE

Step 3: Grasp wraps between thumb and forefinger and slide the know off tip and unto Fly Line. While still holding the wraps, tighten know by gently pulling on both ends of the Leader. Adjust the knot as necessary.

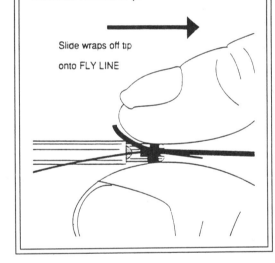

Slide wraps off tip

onto FLY LINE

Nail Knot—Tie Leader to Fly Line

Knot. The Double Clinch Knot runs two lines through the eye and is the strongest knot I know. With practice, it is quick to tie. I refuse to go fishing without a Knot Tyer, and always carry an extra one in my vest. Not that I am inclined to lose things on the river . . .

With the ability to quickly tie great, strong knots, there is no excuse to ever fish with a frayed leader or tippet. Retying is quick and beneficial. One day I hooked and fought a huge male Chinook that, I think, weighed near 30-pounds. I fought him over twenty-two min-

utes—I checked my watch. There was no place to beach him at the rocky run. I tried to tail him several times, but he always eluded my grasp. Finally, on a rush that was not particularly strong, the leader broke. It broke in the 15-pound section of monofilament above the Slinky.

That fish was lost because I had not replaced that section of the leader when I retied. There was no excuse; I had run my fingers down it, in my regular checking procedure, but I was too lazy or too harried to retie. I paid the price. Check often for a frayed leader and tippet and replace it. Do not follow my bad example. Learn from my mistake. I have.

To link the fly line to the leader, we always tie a nail knot. We have lost some great fish because a braided end-loop failed. Tied correctly, a nail knot slides well through the guides during a fight. Though when a fish runs you must let off the pressure as the nail knot goes through your guides. Simply lower the rod tip and feed the knot through the guides. To tail or net your own fish on a long leader, you must reel the nail knot into your guides.

Reviving & Releasing Huge Fish

If you use these techniques to fatigue fish, it is much easier to revive them, because of the short fight. To revive a fish, hold it facing into the current with one hand on its tail and balance the fish with your free hand. Make sure you face the fish *into the current*. Because of the construction of a fish's gills, if you hold it backwards in the current the gills cannot absorb the oxygen. Holding it backwards in the current actually suffocates the fish.

Also lift the fish's mouth out of the water occasionally to let the water and air bubbles run through its gills for a couple seconds before submerging it again. This seems to force oxygen through the gills. Hold the fish in the current until it regains its balance and it can hold itself upright when you release it. Relax your grip on its tail and wait to see if it swims

Mack and Drew Filkins in 1991

away. If anything, take some extra time to revive a fish. Make sure it will survive.

One joy of fishing is teaching the next generation of fishermen. The catch and release ethic is one important item to pass along. Teach the youngsters who fish with you about your catch and release ethic. However, do not force your ethic on them. Let them make up their minds about releasing a fish they catch. One man mentioned how he was spoiled on fishing because his dad forced him to release every fish that he caught as a child.

When my sons first started fishing with me, I would release all the steelhead and salmon on each trip. They tried to convince me to keep them to show their mom. So I taught them why and how to release the fish. I released every hen and kept a male, if I kept any fish at all. I do not enforce my catch and release ethic on my friends, either. If they legally catch a fish, I never protest their keeping it.

So we set up guidelines with my sons for catch and release.

- The person who catches the fish decides the fate of that fish.
- Obviously, no fish can be kept illegally—it must be legally hooked and within the legal limit. No exceptions!
- If you keep a fish, you have to eat it or hang it. Or you must *already* know someone who will eat the fish.
- You cannot ask someone else to keep their fish. If they catch it, they decide its fate. You cannot force your keep or release ethic on another angler. "If you want to keep a fish then *you catch one*."
- You cannot protest anyone else's decision about his fish. Do not give your opinion unless you are asked!

These rules did two things. It gave them the responsibility to decide the fish's fate while displaying the seriousness of keeping a fish. Secondly, it motivated them to catch a fish on their own. If I hooked a fish and let them land it, it was my fish and I decided its fate. Knowing that they had to personally eat a fish or give it to someone who would eat it urged them to consider carefully their decision. Especially since neither of them is a big fan of eating fish.

When they decide to keep a fish that I would release, I respect their decision without discussion or visual disapproval. I would rather watch them keep a fish than steal their joy of fishing. Surprisingly, over the years they have developed their own catch and release ethic that makes their father glad.

One Final Catch

Two weeks after Al Renner lost that male King salmon because it went under the cedar trunk near Ping Pong Alley, he fished that stretch of river again. This time Al hooked a 37-inch hen Chinook from a redd that was only 15 to 20 feet upstream from the downed pop-

lar tree. When Al hooked the fish it immediately turned and charged under the tree, with Al following quickly—well, as quickly as his short legs could carry him.

When Al got to the tree he poked his rod under the tree and straddled the large tree trunk. The tree was too big for his short arms (longer arms wouldn't help much either) to reach the rod tip on the downriver side. So Al picked up the rod tip with his left wader boot, while he still held the rod handle with his right hand. He then let go with his right hand and lifted the rod quickly to his left hand with his boot.

Al then scrambled over the log while moving down the rod hand-over-hand until he got to the cork. When he lifted the rod, the huge hen thrashed on the end of the line. Al then fought the fish down around the now-famous Ping-Pong Alley, and tailed her by himself. I guess Al was wrong that day when he saw me dip the rod under a tree and pull it out the other side. He *was* man enough for this fishing!

Al Renner with a steelhead

Floating Egg Cluster fly

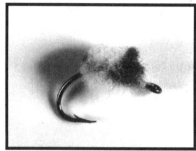

Glo-Bugs Fly

Number 10 Black Stonefly nymph

Latex Wigglers

Green Caddis Larva

Salmon Streamers

Latex Stone nymph

Glow-Nymph

Bunny Leech

Burlap Bug nymph

Woolly Bugger

'arrow-Nymph

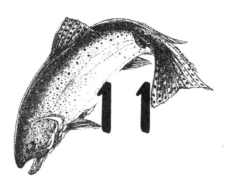

Tying Simple—And Simply Seductive—
Salmon and Steelhead Flies

My most often quoted fishing motto is, "If you're not losing flies, you're not fishing."

With all the obstructions in Great Lakes tributaries, if you are not losing flies to logs, you are not fishing where the steelhead hide—and will not catch many fish. If, like me, you plan to lose many flies while fishing, then the easier and more simple the flies are to tie, the better they are. As long as they are still *seductive*.

Here we will not rehearse the details about steelhead and salmon flies that others have stated elsewhere. Here we will share a selection of twelve flies that *anyone* can tie that will catch steelhead and salmon. I am living proof that even if you have ten thumbs you can still tie these flies. Anyone can tie these flies and though your versions may not be pretty, they will catch fish. Once you learn the skills to tie these twelve flies, you will be surprised by the number of complicated flies you can tie.

When I visit fly shops, I often wonder if flies are not tied to catch fisherman more than to catch fish. If the fisherman does not take the fly, the fish will never get a chance. Once a fly hits the shelf for sale it competes with the other flies on display. It must compete for the angler's take. Maybe the most competition is there in the fly shop before it ever gets to the river.

Though we all would like to tie flies as beautiful as the professionals, their's do not necessarily catch more fish. I often think ugly grubby looking flies even work better. At first my most frequent tying mistake was making flies too big and/or bulky. Bigger is not better—neither in size nor bulk. Scantily tied flies seem to work best. For instance, two wraps of hackle on an 'arrow-Nymph's collar is much better than five wraps. But it was hard to convince myself of that at first.

Along with these twelve successful flies, I will not go to the river without several other flies. These include Oscar's Hex-nymph, Tom

Johnson's P.M. Wiggler, the Sparrow nymph and other time-consuming flies. These twelve flies are quick to tie and inexpensive. They cost as little as 7 to 17 cents *each*—but the hook cost is usually the major expense. Hooks can cost between 2.5 and 15 cents each.

If you learn to tie these flies and tie lots of them, then you may catch more steelhead and salmon than ever before. You will catch more fish, if only because you will not feel badly about losing flies. You will break off flies that get caught in the bushes across the river instead of spooking fish to retrieve "those precious flies." While fishing I constantly break off flies on branches or submerged logs rather than spook the pod of steelhead or salmon we are targeting.

When you can tie your own flies quickly and inexpensively, you will be more inclined to cast into difficult places to catch fish. That too increases the number of steelhead that you hook and catch. If, however, you have unlimited financial resources and can freely buy and lose all the flies you want, then ignore this chapter. If you want to share in the joy of catching a steelhead or trophy salmon on a fly that you tied, then read on.

Don't Worship the God of Exactness

One of my TEN COMMANDMENTS OF FLY TYING is "Don't worship the god of exactness." Do not think that a fly tied with the wrong materials will not catch fish—coincidentally that is why we tie flies *to catch fish.* Another FLY TYING COMMANDMENT is "If the fish accepts a fly, so do I." Steelhead and salmon accept flies that are tied with all kinds of materials substituted for the "traditional materials."

Do you really think a fish can tell the difference between a nymph's wing casing tied with pheasant tail instead of turkey wing? Or can a fish tell the difference between a Spring's Wiggler tied with Fox squirrel tail instead of Gray squirrel tail? Or would a steelhead reject a Woolly Bugger because you bought the ma-

rabou from a craft store instead of paying several times the price at a fly shop? Can a fish tell if you used a russet-colored saddle hackle instead of a brown hen hackle? If the fish don't worship the "god of exactness," neither will I.

Bob Nicholson substitutes items when tying his flies too. Nicholson said, "Kaufman Simulator makes a great stonefly pattern. But a Kaufman Simulator true to pattern will have two goose biots, which are a pain to tie. So I just take scrap hackle, split it in a 'V' and tie it in for the tail. Then I tie a hackle in by the tip, then wrap the peacock herl and tie off the head."

Nicholson also ties what his friends call, "Those darn guide flies." Bob calls them "Nicholson's specials." He said, "That is the generic term for the guide flies I tie because they are quick and dirty. I wrap a hook with rug yarn then take a black marker and draw

Salmon & Steelhead Hooks
Long-shanked hooks #6 & #8:
    Mustad # 36890—Black Salmon
    Mustad # 79580—Viking
    Mustad # 9575—Limerick
    Mustad # 33960—Sprout

Medium-shanked hooks #6 & #8:
    Mustad # 3366—Sprout
    Mustad # 7957BX—a stout hook
    Mustad # 3136
    Mustad # 3399A

Short-shanked hooks #6 & #8:
    Mustad # 80250BR
    Mustad # 9479
    Mustad # 92141
    Mustad # 9523

Wide-gap hooks #6 & #8:
    Mustad # 37160—up eye
    Mustad #37140—straight eye

**Examples of hooks for tying
steelhead and salmon flies**

along the back. I put on a turn of hackle for the collar and it's done. It takes 45 seconds to tie."

Also, I have no conscience about using whatever hooks are available as long as they have a sufficient strength and gap. Generally, I tie all my steelhead and salmon flies on either Number 6 or 8 hooks. I simply tie the length of the shank to the size of the fly. I have some distinct preferences for hooks—some are fly hooks, others are not. For instance, I prefer the black Mustad #36890 Salmon hooks for Woolly Buggers, streamers and 4-Egg Clusters. My favorite Number 10 Stonefly nymph hook was a bait hook. It was a Number 8 worm hook—a bait barb. This Korean made "Comet Hook" had a good gap, nymph-shape and excellent strength. They were very inexpensive, only $2.49 for a box of 100—under 2.5 cents per hook. Unfortunately, I cannot find anyone who currently sells these hooks.

The Perfect Fly
The perfect steelhead and salmon fly is one that has four characteristics.
- It is *easy and quick to tie*
- It simulates and *emulates a natural food* source's profile
- It has *lots of inherent movement* such as philoplume or marabou
- It has fibers that *catch in the fish's teeth*

These dozen flies contain these four qualities in varying degrees.

Floating Egg Cluster fly—tied in 2- egg and 4-egg patterns
Glo-Bugs® fly—tied with Glo-Bugs® yarn
Number 10 Black Stonefly nymph—tied completely with black rug yarn
Latex Wigglers—tied on wide-gap hooks
Green Caddis Larva—tied in at least six colors
Salmon Streamers—tied with buck tail, bear hair or marabou wings
Latex Stone nymph—tied in cream, black and yellow

Glow-Nymph—tied with glow-in-the-dark squid bodies
Woolly Bugger—tied in several variations
Bunny Leech—tied with strips of rabbit fur
Burlap Bug nymph—tied with fibers of a burlap sack
'arrow-Nymph—tied as an imitation Sparrow nymph

Blessed Be The Tyer
When you tie these twelve patterns with variations, they become other fly patterns. For instance, if you replace the Woolly Bugger's marabou tail with a small loop of bright yarn, you create a Woolly Worm. You can also vary these patterns in color and size. With all these variations your fly box will overflow, if you tie a few of each pattern and its variants. I have done just that.

One day while giving away some flies on the river, an angler saw my fly box and asked, "Do you own a fly shop?"

"No," I answered, "I own a fly *vise*."

As you begin to tie these patterns and any other new fly pattern you learn, remember John Kilmer's addition the FLY TYING COMMANDMENTS "You must tie at least seven flies of any new fly pattern before you begin to get the feel of the materials."

Do not get discouraged with your first few flies of any new pattern. Stay with it. It does get easier and the flies do start looking better. Feel free to experiment and invent your own versions of these flies. That is how the 'arrow-Nymph was created. Sparrow nymphs are an excellent pattern but they take some time to tie. So I began tying them with olive chenille and a hen hackle collar. The 'arrow-Nymph has been very successful. The Sparrow nymph is no doubt a better pattern, but the 'arrow-Nymph is much faster to tie. I still always keep several Sparrow nymphs in my box for those reluctant fish I encounter.

The following list includes all the materi-

Fly Tying Materials

Kevlar thread—cream colored
Fly tying thread—black
Needle—a large sewing needle
  (from a sewing kit)
5-mm Pom-Poms—orange and
  yellow (from a craft store)
Yarn—black, cream & olive (Aunt
  Lydia's Rug Yarn, buy it by the
  skein from Walmart)
Saddle hackle—black
Grizzle hen neck hackle or saddle
  hackle
Latex tourniquets—cream colored
  (from a hospital or doctor)
Permanent Markers—black,
  yellow, chartreuse
Chenille (size medium) olive,
  black, brown

Marabou—olive, black, brown
  (from a craft store)
Glo-Bugs® yarn—Neon red,
  chartreuse, natural, your favorite
  colors
Tinsel—small gold and silver tinsel
Squirrel tail—Fox squirrel
  (off a road kill)
Zonker Rabbit strips—black,
  white & olive (from a tanned
  rabbit hide)
Burlap threads—from the lettered
  section of a burlap bag
Pheasant wing or tail—shoot one
(in season) and salt it
Head Cement—or clear fingernail
polish

als needed to tie these twelve flies. Some of these items are non-traditional but they work. If you have never tied flies before, you may want to purchase a basic fly tying kit that includes the essential tools. I also encourage you to buy and use a "whip finish" tool. I never did learn how to use one from the instructions, so I asked a fly tying friend to teach me. It was well worth the effort.

Fly vise—My friend Gary Agle created a homemade version of a fly vise with a pair of needle-nose Vise-Grip® pliers, a C-clamp, a metal rod and a welder. The metal rod is welded to the top of the C-clamp then the pliers are welded (on an angle) to the top of the six-inch rod. Before you weld on the pliers, remove the spring because the heat of the welding will ruin the spring. Replace the spring once the pliers have cooled. I own an expensive 360° rotating, Renzetti® fly vise but I almost exclusively use my homemade one.

Hooks—Buy Number 6 and 8 hooks, in different shank lengths and get some a wide-gap hooks. See page 118 for examples of hooks and lengths, but once you become familiar with the length of each category, please feel free to experiment with different hooks. Once I got a great deal on nearly two thousand Number 6 Sproat hooks (medium shanked and straight eyed). Honestly, I doubted the hardiness and strength of that hook. But I tied many flies on it and landed *lots* of steelhead and salmon with it, including my largest fish ever.

Glo-Bugs® Flies
#6 or #8 Short hook
Glo-Bugs® yarn
Kevlar thread
First lay on the thread down to the middle of the shank. Cut a short piece of yarn (your favorite color) then lay it on the hook and wrap it in the middle with three wraps of thread. Pull up the yarn and wrap thread behind and in front of the yarn, then tie off. Then pull up *all* of the yarn and cut in a semicircle. Also, tie a few flies very scarcely in natural colored yarn with a splash of orange or red. That is a great redd fly.

Glo-Bugs® Fly ▸

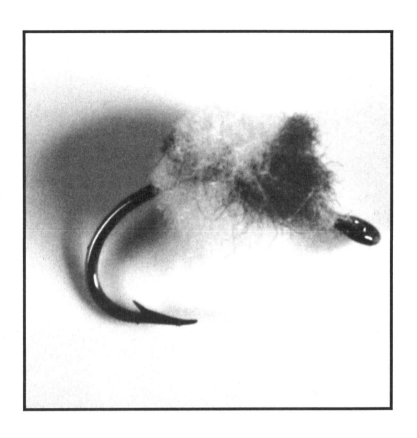

**Number 10 Black
Stonefly Nymph**
#8 Short hook
Black rug yarn
Black thread
Separate Aunt Lydia's Rug yarn into strands. Lay the thread on the hook and go at least ¾ the way around the shank. Use the end of a long strand to tie on a short tail. Build the body by wrapping the rest of the tail strand half way up the hook shank. Tie two short strands of yarn for the wing casing, then wrap the tail strand to create the thorax. Cut two short strands of yarn and lay them on top of the thorax. Wrap them with an "X" of thread so that they stick out each side of the thorax. Pull down the wing casing and tie if off. Trim the legs to length.

Number 10 Black Stonefly Nymph ▲

Latex Wiggler Fly
#6 or #8 Wide-gap hook
Latex strips 3/8-inch wide
(cut from medical tourniquets)
Saddle hackle
Squirrel tail

Lay the thread down almost to the bend then tie in a squirrel tail. Tie in the tip of a hackle, then tie on a strip of latex. Wrap latex up hook, then lay seven wraps of hackle up to the eye. Then tie it off.

◀ **Latex Wiggler Fly**

Salmon Streamers
#6 or #8 Long hook
Wing material—bucktail, marabou, bear hair, or squirrel tail
Body material—gold or silver tinsel or chenille

Tie in tinsel (or chenille) at the bend and wrap it to the front. Tie it off and put on a wing (the length of the hook shank) and tie it off.

Salmon Streamers ▶

Green Caddis Larva
#6 or #8 Short hook
Olive yarn

Tie in olive yarn ¾ of the way around the hook and wrap it to the eye and tie it off. Tie this in several shades of green, including chartreuse. Also some Great Lakes tributaries have black Caddis, and a Black Caddis fly is very effective. One option is to put a couple wraps of peacock herl for a head.

Green Caddis Larva ▶

Latex Stonefly Nymphs
#6 Medium hook
Latex strips—3/8-inch wide
Squirrel tail
Hen or saddle hackle

Tie in a short tail of squirrel or marabou, then tie in latex strip and wrap the body half way up the shank. Tie in the wing casing and hackle, then wrap the latex for the thorax. Wrap the hackle, lay down the wing and tie it off. With a permanent marker you can create a black or yellow stonefly. When you do, leave a small unmarked section under the thorax. Dig a rotten log out of the river and look at the stone flies' thorax, to mimic that spot on a stonefly's thorax. This pattern can be tied on a Number 10 hook to create a small Black Stonefly nymph.

Latex Stonefly Nymphs ▲

Glow-Nymphs
#6 Medium hook
Squirrel tail
Hen or saddle hackle
Glow-in-the-dark squid bodies

Tie this Glow-Nymph just like the previous nymph except that you can use squid legs in place of the latex for the body and thorax. Also, do not use a marker on these flies.

Glow-Nymphs ▶

Woolly Buggers ▼

Woolly Buggers
#6 or #8 Long hook
Marabou
Saddle hackle
Chenille

Tie in shank-length marabou for the tail, then tie in chenille and the tip of hackle at the hook's bend. Wrap the chenille to the eye, then wrap the hackle and tie it off. Adding tinsel to the tail and body creates a Flash-A-Bugger. Replace the marabou tail with a short loop of bright yarn to create a Woolly Worm. If you tie in squirrel as a tail (to replace the marabou), and pull the squirrel over the shank (as a full-body wing-casing), you get a Spring Wiggler. If you use Glo-Bugs® yarn (chartreuse) in place of the squirrel tail, use a neon chenille (red) and bright hackle (chartreuse) and you create a Neon Wiggler.

Floating Egg Cluster Fly
#6 Medium hook—4-Egg fly
#6 Short hook—2-Egg fly
Kevlar thread—cream
5-mm Pom-Poms—orange and
    yellow
Sewing needle—large

Thread Kevlar onto a needle and run the needle through 12 Pom-Poms, alternating colors. Remove needle, then lay thread on hook shank back to the bend; hold a Pom-Pom 3/8-inch above the hook shank. Wrap Kevlar over, in front and behind the threads from the Pom-Pom so it remains suspended. Wrap the thread up the shank and lay the next Pom-Pom directly on the hook shank. Repeat process with the 4-Egg Cluster, then whip finish (or half-hitch). Cement the knot. Kevlar thread is the best for this fly because of its toughness, especially when the eggs get caught in the fish's teeth.

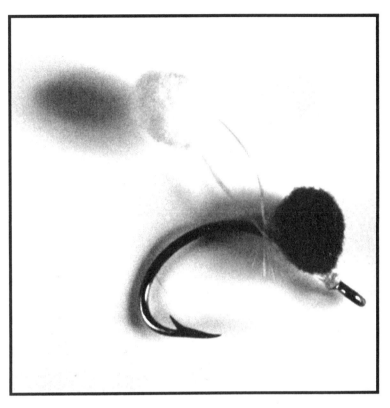

Floating Egg Cluster Fly ▲

Bunny Leeches

#6 Long hook
Zonker strips—olive, white
    or black

Tie in a rabbit strip creating a ¾-inch tail, then wrap the strip up the length of the shank and tie it off. This is also a great pattern for Northern pike and smallmouth bass.

◀ **Bunny Leeches**

Burlap Bug nymph

#6 or #8 Medium hook
Squirrel tail
Pheasant wing or tail
Hen or saddle hackle
Burlap threads

Tie this nymph just like a latex nymph except you replace the latex with the burlap thread. Use the threads from where the bag is printed. This fly imitates a Hex-nymph, a mayfly nymph and a stonefly nymph.

◀ **Burlap Bug nymph**

'arrow-Nymph
an imitation Sparrow nymph

#6 Medium Sproat hook
Olive chenille
Grizzle hen hackle

Tie in the olive chenille at the bend, leaving 3/8-inch hanging back as a tail. Wrap the rest of the chenille up the shank then add two wraps of hen hackle and tie it off.

'arrow-Nymph ▶

Epilogue

Spring and Fall

Now for the big question about all the details and techniques in this book. Do they really work? Is it really that simple? Or, is this an oversimplification? Can *anyone* learn to catch salmon and steelhead? Is there enough evidence here to guide fishermen to consistently catch these migrants?

The spring and fall following the completion of this manuscript (except for this Chapter) we had an opportunity to test the premise of this book on both the spring steelhead run and the fall salmon run. We tested these principles and techniques on two different Great Lakes tributaries, in two different countries. They were also tested by fishermen with a great variety of fishing experience.

The spring crew included: Byron Reinhold (from Indiana), his son Paul Reinhold, Paul's father-in-law Frank Stidham (both from Ohio), Bill Garland (a Texan we met at a local RV

Park), Al Renner and Tom McNerney (my friends from downstate Michigan) and my physician and friend, Jaak Pahn (from the Sault). Their fishing experience ranged from a complete fly fishing neophyte to a world-traveling fly fisherman. Some had vast fishing experience in other types of fishing, some had rarely ever fished.

In the spring, we fished an Ontario tributary of Lake Huron, on a stretch that was downriver of the primary spawning area. This heavily fished stretch had a fast, deep run which included some spawning gravel (deep water redds) then it ran into a deep, dark pool that split around an island before it continued downriver. We fished for ten days over the next two and a half weeks, and the number of fishermen varied from two to five. In those ten days we landed 93 steelhead, three of those days we landed over 14 fish. One fish was 15.5-pounds, which would have won the local fishing contest by over 3.5-pounds. But we released it.

One Canadian fisherman was so amazed at the effectiveness of the flies and techniques that he asked, "What flies are you guys using? How are you casting them? You are the only ones fishing this whole river that are *fair-hooking* steelhead. The rest are foul-hooking fish." At that we educated yet another angler to these techniques. After the first few days the fly fishing guides were asking our party for hints and tips for catching the steelhead on *their* river.

The principles and techniques we shared are simply the ones previously included. The two most effective flies for those days were the *Hexegenia Navatalovia* ("a female Hexnymph on steroids") which is a bulky Hexnymph tied with a cream colored marabou tail (like a Woolly Bugger), and an olive colored P.M. Wiggler ("Is there any river where that fly will *not* catch fish?").

We taught Bill Garland the Drift-fly fishing and were amazed how quickly he became a effective caster. We wondered if his Texan bass jigging helped him, but he later admitted using a similar casting technique while fishing in Alaska. We found that casting and hooking came naturally to Bill, but fighting the steelhead was a challenge, especially since he had to scramble downriver over rocky terrain to land the fish in the deep pool.

> *After a few days the fly fishing guides were asking our party for hints for catching the steelhead on their river*

We found several of the techniques were especially applicable to our situation those days. First we had to use long, long tippets. The length from the fly line to the last fly was often 20-feet. It was ten or eleven feet to the Slinky Drifter then six or seven feet to the first fly and three or four feet between the flies. On one sunny afternoon before the rest arrived, I

went "just to check out the river conditions" (I did not expect to see any fish on this bright afternoon). I did see steelhead holding in the deep runs. Several fishermen cast to visible fish throughout the run and pool, so I asked one angler if I could fish below him. He consented. I tied on a very long tippet, with a Hexnymph and an olive Woolly Bugger for the flies. In the next three and a half hours while fishing different stretches of that run, I hooked over 24 steelhead and landed (and released) six.

> *We have no clear idea just how many fish we hooked, fought and lost during those days*

Over the next two weeks we learned a vast amount about where the fish hold in that stretch of river. We dubbed one slot the "9-hole" because it took a Slinky Drifter with 9-weights in it to get the flies down in that fast, deep cut. We learned how to spot steelhead holding in the deep runs and near undercut banks. The largest steelhead, at 15½-pounds, was hooked and landed after it was spotted holding in a very deep run where he and three other steelhead simply looked like shadows of rocks. Once spotted it was necessary to wade out into fast, chest-deep water to get into the correct position to cast to these fish. It also took a "9-hole" slinky to get the flies down into the strike zone. Once hooked the steelhead turned and swam down into the deep pool. He was fought there for twenty minutes before he submitted to pressure and was netted in the slack water to the side of the pool.

Those days were the greatest steelhead fishing any of us had ever had.

Fall. . . A King's Delight

The following fall we again tested the techniques and principles of this book on the run of Chinook salmon. The fall testing team that gathered included Byron Reinhold ("there are

Joe Cloud with a 35-pound King Salmon

river because it bleeds out into a shallow marsh a few miles before the takeout spot. The river's main branch splits into countless fingers and rivulets, making it tough to know which to take. All of the rivulets are shallow and we had to walk the boat through much of the swamp. But the up-side is that we found some great pools, and even a few redds.

In the two and a half days we saw only one other fisherman, who owned a cabin on that stretch of river. We soon became friends and he fished with us. We fished about halfway between the classic spawning area and the mouth of the river. Our trip was *during* the migration of the Chinooks, so we often saw Kings swimming up river as we fished or drifted. We looked for pools as I described in the chapters on summer and fall steelhead and for the salmon runs. Not every pool held fish every day, but each day we were able to find the best pools for that day.

Every day we cast to very fresh, happy Chinook salmon that were only a day or two out of the big lake. The best and most consistent pool was found by the "Hole Boss," Bill Garland, and we dubbed that pool the "5-Minute Hole." It was a classic resting pool where the salmon stopped as they migrated. With a casual glance this pool could easily be passed over as you drift down river. I definitely would have drifted past it except the Hole Boss insisted that we fish it.

It was a nondescript pool that resulted from the confluence of two branches of the river which had been separated by a small island. It had a 1/3-mile long stretch of shallow water above and below the pool. This made it a rest-

some advantages to being retired"), and Bill Garland returned from Texas and brought along his friend Joe Cloud. I met them on the river and the four of us fished together for two and a half days.

We chose mid-September for the rendezvous. The traditional spawning area of a Lake Michigan tributary was choked with fisherman. The banks were lined with anglers and people flogged every pool and redd from sunrise to dark. We sought out a new stretch of river to fish. We found a stretch where we did not see another boat for the whole float, which took *all* day. None of the guides float that stretch of ing spot for *every* salmon that migrated past us. The pool did not look very deep, but it was between eight and twelve feet deep in the center. It ran from the point of the island and tapered off toward the opposite bank, where the salmon often held under the overhanging trees.

In those days we *landed* over 80 Chinook salmon; all were in perfect condition except for a few with sea lamprey scars. The size and strength of these Kings was amazing. We caught a few fish under 10-pounds but most were over 18-pounds and several of fished measured over 40-inches. Fighting and netting these brutes proved to be a challenge every time one was hooked. We have no clear idea just how many fish we hooked, fought and lost during those days.

The first day, Joe Cloud hooked a huge King in the "5-Minute Hole" and it charged upstream to the right side of the island. Cloud followed it and I followed him as he struggled to keep the fish within the "45° rule." The water in that side of the island was four to five feet deep, but it was cluttered with sticks and logs protruding from the bottom. Soon this fish got the fly line rapped around a submerged branch.

"Hey, this fish has you around a branch, just like the one Byron had here twenty minutes ago," I said, reminding Joe of the fish that Byron had fought up this same branch and then lost when Byron fought it back into the pool where it broke the 8-pound tippet.

"Well, dive down and get my fly line off the branch like you did for Byron," Joe said, "You can't get any more wet!"

When Byron fought his fish upriver, I waded to close to the head of the pool and went "swimming" in my waders. Joe pulled me out by grabbing the net I held. So when Byron's line got caught around a submerged branch in the middle of the current, I reached down and unhooked Joe's line from the branch so Byron could fight the fish again.

Since I was still soaking wet,

Byron Reinhold

Joe saw no reason I could not do the same thing for him. I did.

Joe's fish then fought him back into the pool, and after several minutes it charged out of the pool again—downriver this time. Fortunately, Joe was able to fight it away from two sets of logs as it led him downriver. I waded ahead of Joe and the fish to net it when it tired. Two hundred yards down river, I tried to net it three times but could not keep it in the net. When I tried twice to grab its huge tail, it eluded me. The next time I grabbed for its tail I heard loud snap and a louder gasp. Joe's rod had broken a few inched above the cork.

"Grab the top section!" I yelled, "I'll try to grab him quickly." I knew our chances to land this fish were now greatly reduced and getting worse.

Joe held his onto broken rod and line, as I put the net in front of the fish then reached to grab its tail. As the fish backed away from the net I grabbed its tail. When it felt my hand it swam forward into the net. With that I picked it out of the water. Then we realized how huge this male King was. It measured 43.5-inches long with a girth of over 25.5-inches, and it weighed 35.3-pounds.

As we dislodged the olive P.M. Wiggler from his mouth we found another fly in his tongue. It was Byron's 'arrow-Nymph, that he had lost on a huge King twenty minutes before Joe hooked his fish. Then we realized that Joe's

The "Hole Boss"—Bill Garland

fish was the *same* Chinook Byron had fought and lost.

"Hey, Joe, you know that Byron should get to hang that fish half of the year on his wall in Indiana," Bill Garland said, ribbing Joe, "Without Byron tiring out that huge male, you would have never landed it."

"Yes, and I netted and tailed it, so I should get to hang it in my office, for four months a year," I chimed in with a smile.

"You're right, Kenn, and I should get to hang it at my house, because Joe wouldn't even be here without me inviting him, picking him up from the airport . . ." Bill continued.

"So I get it four months a year," Byron summed up, "Then Kenn gets it for the next four. And Bill gets it for the final four months each year."

"And Joe—you get the photos and the memories!" Bill said with his Texan smile.

"As much as I *appreciate* you guys and all your help," Joe rebuffed, "This fish will go on my pharmacy wall, but you all are welcome to come see him anytime you want."

Joe's pharmacy wall has mounts of whitetail deer, largemouth bass, and full-body mounts of turkey. Now that Chinook salmon hangs on Joe's pharmacy wall in Texas, along with his broken rod, a photo, and the Master Angler patch from the Michigan Department of Natural Resources.

On Bill Garland's wall hangs a female Chinook which weighed over 33-pounds. But as stories often do in Texan, these fish are probably much larger now then when they were in Michigan. Remember, "Everything is larger in Texas." Rumor now has it that two Texans came to Michigan one fall and each took home 50-plus pound Chinook salmon.

Bill became so focused on landing a fish larger that Joe's that he went to extreme lengths to land salmon. As Byron fought a huge, fresh fish up the left branch of the island, another salmon (for some inexplicable reason) swam out of the pool and beached itself in some shallow, black muck on the island. Bill charged over there with his net to land what he thought was Byron's fish. It alluded him for several minutes as the rest of us landed Byron's fish then sat down laughing at Garland trying to capture this elusive, now-black salmon. It squirmed away from Bill every time he got close to it, but it never left the black muck. Finally Bill got on his hands and knees to chase the fish which splattered him with black muck every time he reached out for her.

Finally she conceded and he caught her. But our consensus was that the fish "won," and we

could not conceal our delight that she had flung mud on the "Hole Boss." Served him right as far as we were concerned. . .

Passing The Test

Again this trip confirmed the techniques and premise of this book. These fresh Chinook wanted little to do with bright flies or egg patterns. They wanted *nymphy-looking* flies and olive was their favorite color. P.M. Wigglers, 'arrow-Nymphs, Woolly Buggers, Caddis Larva and Hex-nymphs were the most successful flies.

We found again that very long tippets worked the best in the fall, even while fishing pools. Mostly we used 8-pound-test tippet, but the Texans sometimes used 10-pound. In the deep pool the 10-pound test seemed to work fine, but I still believe that we got more strikes on 8-pound test.

> *Very long tippets worked the best in the fall, even while fishing pools*

Finding "resting pools" was a key ingredient to the success. But it was not as hard as we thought, even on a new stretch of river. The day after Byron and I left for home, Bill and Joe fished the 5-Minute Hole for the last time. Bill said that they only had one strike all morning and that they were ready to pack it in. But around noon, they saw several wakes created by migrating salmon swimming up river. A half hour later the 5-Minute Hole was stacked with over two dozen fresh salmon.

"Then we could not get our flies down through the pool without hooking a fish," Bill told me over the phone. "It was the most unbelievable thing I have ever seen. I don't know how many fish we hooked, fought and landed that afternoon. But we kept two salmon over 40-inches to take back to Texas whole, otherwise who would ever believe *us*?"

"You got a point there," I kidded him.

Where to go from here?

On our final day together that fall, we said our goodbyes and spoke of when we would meet again.

"What do you think, Joe?" Bill asked, "How did you like your first trip to fish Great Lakes rivers?"

"A fisherman could never get too much of this," Joe smiled, as I realized these are two men who have and can fish Alaska or any place they choose.

"Where shall we fish next spring and fall?" Bill continued, "Shall we go back to Alaska?"

"You can go to Alaska if you want, Bill," Joe said quickly, "But I'm coming back to Michigan . . ."

Knot Tying

(Clinch Knot and Nail Knot shown on pages 112 and 113)

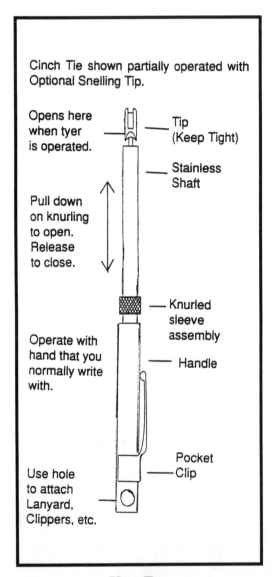

Cinch Tie shown partially operated with Optional Snelling Tip.

Opens here when tyer is operated.

Tip (Keep Tight)

Stainless Shaft

Pull down on knurling to open. Release to close.

Knurled sleeve assembly

Operate with hand that you normally write with.

Handle

Pocket Clip

Use hole to attach Lanyard, Clippers, etc.

Knot Tyer

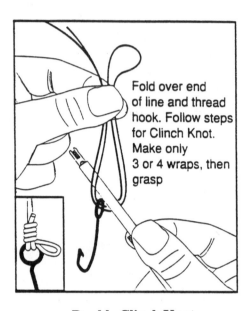

Fold over end of line and thread hook. Follow steps for Clinch Knot. Make only 3 or 4 wraps, then grasp

Double Clinch Knot

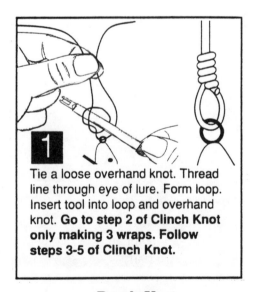

1 Tie a loose overhand knot. Thread line through eye of lure. Form loop. Insert tool into loop and overhand knot. **Go to step 2 of Clinch Knot only making 3 wraps. Follow steps 3-5 of Clinch Knot.**

Rapala Knot

Glossary

Barrel Swivel—A small swivel shaped like a barrel with a ring on each end.

Buggy Patterns (of flies)—A style of tying flies that "resemble" acquatic insects.

Butt Leader (for Drift-fly-fishing)—The monofilament from the fly line (or shooting line) down to the barrel swivel.

Caddis Larva—One of any larva of the several species of aquatic insects called Caddis.

Dead-drifting (a Fly)—Drifting a fly down stream so it appears unattached to any line.

Dead-drift Zone—The area in the current where you try to keep the fly from being pulled to the side by your leader.

Deep-nymphing—Using weights (split-shot or Slinky drifters) to drift nymphs deep in the current when a weighted fly could not get down.

Drag—The sideways movement of the fly in the current because of the pull of the line.

Drag-free Drift—The amount of distance a fly drifts down river before the line begins to pull it to the side.

Foul-hooking (a fish)—Accidentally hooking a fish anywhere but in the mouth.

Fishing blind—Fishing a pool of a river where you cannot see the fish you are trying to catch.

Gap (of a hook)—The distance from the hook point up to the shank (the long straight section) of the hook.

Glo bugs—Bright, colorful flies tied with bright yarn especially created for salmon fishing.

Hole (of a river)—A deep, slow section of river, usually at a bend in the river; same as a "pool."

Leader—The monofilament from the fly line to the flies.

Leader (for Drift-fly-fishing)—The monofilament from the fly line (or shooting line) to the barrel swivel.

Migration (of salmon or steelhead)—The journey of salmon and steelhead out of the ocean or Great Lakes back into the natal streams and rivers so they can spawn.

Naturals—The aquatic insects that naturally inhabit a particular stretch of river.

Nymph—The young of an aquatic insect before its metamorphosis into an adult.

Philoplume—The soft webby feathers found behind a pheasant body feather; used on flies to simulate the gills of various aquatic nymphs.

Pod—A school of migrating salmon or steel head as they journey up river to spawn.

Pool (of a river)—Same as a holding "hole" for migrating fish; a deep, slow section of river, usually at a bend in the river.

Redd—A gravel shelf in the river bottom where the salmon or steelhead hollow out an indentation to lay its eggs; where steelhead and salmon spawn; for other species of fish they are called "spawning beds."

Reflex Strikes—The instinctive response of a salmon or steelhead to bite a natural nymph or an artificial fly when it drifts in front of its face.

Run (of a river)—A fast flowing section of the current where fish hide during spawning or migration, many times located near a gravel redd.

Shootingheads—A short (three to 30-foot long) section of "special application" fly line; sometimes sinking, but others are floating.

Shooting flyline—Very thin fly line or thick monofilament used with shootingheads; their thin diameter allows for long distance casting.

Sight fishing—Fishing for steelhead or salmon on a redd, run, or pool where the angler can see the fish and/or watch their reaction to the flies.

Sinktip (flylines)—A floating fly line with a section of sinking fly line on its end.

Slinky Drifters—Camouflaged parachute cord with lead balls inserted and melted on each end; used as a weight to pull the flies down to the proper depth.

Snap Swivel—A barrel swivel with a metal snap connected to one of its rings.

Spey Rods—A long fly rod used to cast long distances; most popular with Atlantic salmon fishing.

Spey flies—Flies that are generally known for their very long, webby hackle.

Split shot—Lead weight with a slot cut in them so they may be crimped onto monofilament line.

Streamer (flies)—Flies tied to imitate bait fish of the rivers.

Strike—When a fish bites a fly or lure.

Strike Indicator—A piece of yarn, cork or foam attached to a leader that helps detect a strike.

Strike zone—The area in a drift that the fly is most likely to solicite a bite.

Sulunar calendar—A calendar that determines the most likely time each day (or days of the month) when the fish are most likely to bite.

Tippet—The monofilament tied to the end of the leader then to a fly; in Drift-fly-fishing it's the monofilament between the barrel swivel and the fly(s).

Index